Living Tradition

The Architecture and Urbanism
of Hugh Petter

TRIGLYPH
BOOKS

Living Tradition

The Architecture and Urbanism of Hugh Petter

Written by
Clive Aslet

Photography by
Dylan Thomas

Foreword by
HRH The Former Prince of Wales

TRIGLYPH
BOOKS

Page 4/5: A Stone House outside London
Page 6/7: Chettle House in Dorset
Page 8/9: The Levine Building, Trinity College in Oxford
Page 10/11: Tregunnel Hill, Newquay in Cornwall

CONTENTS

15 FOREWORD
   By HRH The Former Prince of Wales

16 INTRODUCTION

NEW HOUSES

30   A Stone House outside London
44   Bear Ash, Berkshire
56   Stanton Farm, Wiltshire
62   Pembroke House, Paradise Island, Bahamas
72   A House in the Channel Islands

RESTORATION

84   Chettle House, Dorset
112   Fawler Manor, Oxfordshire
128   Old Rectory, Berkshire
140   British School at Rome, Italy
150   A House in Hampshire
168   Sawmill Cottage, Yorkshire
180   Meadow Farm, Jersey

PUBLIC ARCHITECTURE

200   The Levine Building, Trinity College, Oxford
216   Millennium Gate, Atlanta, USA
224   Stocks Golf Clubhouse, Hertfordshire
234   196a Piccadilly, London

MASTERPLANNING & URBAN DESIGN

244   Nansledan and Tregunnel Hill, Cornwall
274   Park View, Oxfordshire
286   The Duchy of Cornwall Estate, Kennington

300   SEEING POTENTIAL
306   CATALOGUE RAISONNÉ
316   ACKNOWLEDGEMENTS
318   PICTURE CREDITS

CLARENCE HOUSE

It gives me the greatest possible pleasure and pride to write this foreword to *Living Tradition*, celebrating the Architecture and Urbanism of Hugh Petter, not least because Hugh was one of the first students on my original Summer School in Civic Architecture in 1990, then senior tutor at my Institute of Architecture shortly afterwards and is now master-planner and architect for the Duchy of Cornwall's urban extension to Newquay, Nansledan. Like many students daring to study traditional architecture in the 1980's, it must have taken great courage to pursue this path with such dedication and I am so very pleased to have been able to offer Hugh, and other students alike, a place where they could study and teach the principles of timeless, traditional architecture and building crafts.

What is clear from this visually satisfying publication is the humility required on the one hand to learn from local traditions and materials in the new-build work and, on the other, in restoration work, the skill to understand the existing structures in their context to see where they could be restored and enhanced to sit harmoniously together. This approach requires a high degree of respect and humility by the architect to cherish the best of what has gone before and update it for contemporary use.

The final section on "Seeing Potential" acts as a perfect summary for Hugh's illustrious career and, captured in the before and after images of the Oval Cricket ground, is the affliction of self-conscious originality versus the love and reverence for the architecture of the past in order to create a building of care, beauty and unintended originality. I can only imagine it takes a great deal of skill and effort to make something appear so effortless.

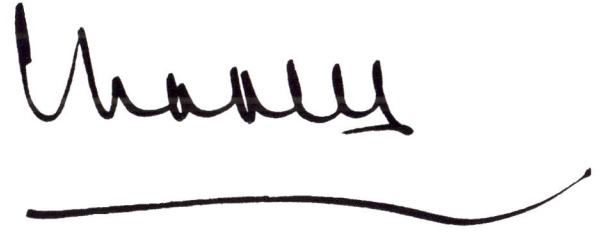

INTRODUCTION

This is a book about the architecture of Hugh Petter, now one of the most senior architects at ADAM Architecture. Hugh's career has been remarkable. Deeply imbued with Classicism, his style is informed by the two years he spent studying Roman buildings and urbanism at the British School at Rome. But his devotion to Vignola, Palladio and Gibbs does not preclude an equal attachment to the Arts and Crafts movement, seen in the time he has spent putting the Art Workers' Guild back on its feet. His respect for materials and craftsmanship is a thread that can be traced throughout his work.

For all his intimate and scholarly knowledge of Classicism, Hugh does not plaster his buildings with ornament. His architecture is self-effacing: the best compliment to pay him is to think one of his buildings has always been there. Much of his practice is concerned with country houses, whether restored and remodelled or built from new. But his reach is longer than that. Not only has he added a substantial range to an Oxford college, but he is responsible for the masterplan of Nansledan, the Duchy of Cornwall's extension to Newquay – a development which shows that it is possible to build sustainably, support the local economy and provide homes where people will form communities to which they will, it is hoped, be attached for decades. He is a cheerleader for the Landowner Legacy movement which, inspired by the Duchy's example, encourages estate owners to build new housing for the long term. In Atlanta, Georgia, he has designed (in collaboration) a triumphal arch that is one of the largest public monuments built in the United States since the Second World War.

What is the element which, for Hugh, unites the different elements of his practice? Above all, it is a deep awareness of tradition. Hence the title of this book. For him, Classicism can be a living language, as is the vernacular of country villages and seaside towns. A detailed study that Hugh made of Lutyens' British School at Rome led him, years later, to extend the building in the manner, not just of Lutyens, but also of its ultimate inspiration, Sir Christopher Wren's St Paul's Cathedral in London. Outside Newquay, the Duchy of Cornwall's Nansledan development sparkles with coloured walls and Art Deco seahorses, derived from the holiday architecture of the Cornish coast. Human beings are creatures of habit who feel comfortable with what they have been brought up with. Over centuries, trial and sometimes error have improved mankind's understanding of how buildings work best – why ignore the wisdom accumulated over so many past generations?

Tall and confident, Hugh could have walked out of a portrait by Gainsborough – a captain in Nelson's navy perhaps. This is not inappropriate. Classical architects have their battles to fight, given the prejudice against them that still exists in some corners of the planning system and architectural establishment. But there is art in his background: his mother Eve's antecedents include the landscape painters James Leakey and Josiah Wood Whymper, as well as Edward Whymper who was the first man to climb the Matterhorn. Hugh's father, Michael, was a civil servant (by training an historian) whose family engineering firm, Petters Limited, founded the Westland Aircraft Works in 1915. Combine art and engineers and the result is architecture. So it proved in Hugh's case at least.

Left: Hugh Petter in the doorway to the addition he built onto his home, Ivy Cottage, in Hampshire. The brickwork, tile hanging and wooden hood above the door, capped in lead, show his love of materials.

He was brought up among paintings, antiques, beautiful houses and gardens.

But a civil service salary did not run to public school for Hugh and his brother John; instead, they were sent to a comprehensive. Having done less well than expected he fell back on his second choice of course at Portsmouth Polytechnic. Unkindly described as the only northern city in the south of England, Portsmouth cannot have offered great inspiration to an aspiring Classical architect. But Hugh was luckier than he might have known at the time of taking up the place, because of the enlightened attitude of the professor in charge of the Architecture School, Geoffrey Broadbent. Unlike many in architectural education, Broadbent was not a dogmatist. Instead, he believed that students should be exposed to as many approaches as possible so that they could choose which suited them best. Modernists taught there but so did the architectural historian Peter Hodson, who had been a pupil of the Modernist bête noire, David Watkin. Through Peter Hodson it was the only architectural school in the UK which taught the Orders as part of the curriculum. The five years that he spent in the trenches at Portsmouth were, he remembers, 'quite hard' and Hodson played a pivotal role in supporting Hugh through that period. Some tutors thought that traditional design was morally wrong and his thesis project for his second degree, for a new Library at Gray's Inn, was marked down from a distinction to a borderline fail at the final internal exam by dogmatic Modernist tutors who divided their time between Portsmouth and the Architectural Association in London. The external examiner then revised the grade back up to a distinction. 'It is quite amusing now, but it certainly wasn't at the time', recalls Hugh.

As chairman of the student architectural society Hugh was responsible for inviting guest lecturers to Portsmouth. One of them was Robert Adam, then establishing his reputation as a traditionalist who married Classical design principles with modern construction methods. In 1987, Hugh joined the firm of which Adam was a director, Winchester Design (the firm changed its name to ADAM

Architecture in 2010). 'I was attracted to working with Bob originally because I admired his fresh thinking on tradition,' remembers Hugh. 'I shared his view that traditions are living things: they adapt and change over time.' It was the beginning of a friendship and professional relationship that has lasted for over thirty years.

A turning point in Hugh's life came in Rome. He had won a scholarship to study for a year at the British School there. This had not been easy to obtain. On his first attempt, made while he was still at Portsmouth, he encountered his old enemy in the form of the Modernist establishment, which dominated the selection panel. His proposal to examine the development of Rome in the late 19th century when it became the capital of a newly united monarchical Italy was condemned as morally wrong. Consequently he was rejected in favour of a candidate of more fashionable views. Fortunately for Hugh, before the victorious candidate could take up his award he was offered a teaching position at the Architectural Association, which he accepted. Hugh received a phone call asking if he would like to be the Rome Scholar instead? 'Yes please' was his response.

This coincided with an initiative of The Prince of Wales, launched after his Mansion House speech in 1987 bemoaning Britain's dismal record of urban development since the Second World War. To encourage a better understanding of tradition among architectural students, his advisors Jules Lubbock and Brian Hanson proposed holding a summer school. It would last a month and a half with three weeks at Magdalen College, Oxford, two at the British School at Rome and one at the Villa Lante to the north of Rome.

Left: (Top left) Hugh teaching a student to do measured drawing on the Dean's Staircase at St. Paul's Cathedral, London, around 1994. (Top right) Hugh measuring the Lutyens façade at the British School at Rome in 1998. Five years later he returned to create a new auditorium and more library space.

Above: A watercolour sketch of Corfu. For Hugh, drawing and watercolours are more than professional tools: they are part of the way he sees the world, even on holiday.

'Portsmouth, to their credit, actually sponsored me to get a place on that first summer school,' remembers Hugh, 'and it was a life-changing moment. After five years at Portsmouth, where I had been largely isolated in terms of ideology and interests, I was suddenly pitched into a global community of twenty-five students who were all passionately interested in traditional architecture. The distinguished group of tutors for the summer school were drawn from across the globe and included such key figures as Leon Krier, David Watkin and Christopher Alexander.'

Two weeks after the end of the summer school Hugh was back in Rome on his Rome Scholarship. This lasted a year, at the end of which he applied again; this time he was successful on his own merits. It helped that he had made a mark in the School, using the Italian he had acquired to take other students on trips into the Campania and generally help them get the most out of their time in Rome. He was also on hand when The Prince of Wales wanted to organise another summer school with a Roman dimension. During the course of this he got to know the supremely urbane journalist Colin Amery. Hugh had long admired Colin, whom he knew through his father's copy of the Financial Times. 'Colin had an extraordinary ability to write eloquently about architecture of any kind and I got my father to photocopy his articles each week so that I could refer to them later.' Teaching on that second summer school led to Hugh being offered the post of senior tutor for the new foundation course at The Prince of Wales's Institute of Architecture (POWIA).

Right: Ivy Cottage in Hampshire. To extend his listed home, Hugh added an extension of two cross-gable roofs in the traditional manner. The materials were picked to harmonise with the existing building, with tiles from Kent and a blend of three bricks laid in Flemish bond.

Following page: The Prince of Wales opens the Levine Building at Trinity College, Oxford, in May 2022. The Former Prince, now His Majesty King Charles III, walks in the centre. To his left is the college President, Dame Hilary Boulding.

At the same time, Thomas Gordon Smith offered him a junior professorship at Notre Dame on their Rome programme. A third year at Rome was an attractive prospect, but Hugh resisted what might have become a life of *dolce fa niente*. It was time to go back to England – initially to teach.

The Foundation Course at POWIA was not intended to compete with mainstream education but to offer something different. Half the students were school age, half of them were mature, half from the UK, half from overseas. 'It was an extraordinary cross section of people and very intensive – 9am until 9pm, five days a week. Everyone who taught there was part time: the objective was to secure the very best people to teach each element of the course. Each project was taught by tutors from different disciplines. Projects require so many people to bring them to fruition: you have to be able to work as part of a team and to understand how to get the best out of people.' All this gave Hugh the training that he had not had as a student. As ever, it was the contacts made with remarkable and creative individuals, such as the dazzling watercolourist Alexander Creswell, which proved so stimulating. To the students, the approach was inspirational. 'We undertook projects where we made and built oak frame buildings; students could follow a project from concept through to actual construction on a building site – for them it was a fantastic experience and gave them an inner confidence which they took with them when they went on elsewhere. They became great apostles for the course and would go on into the schools of architecture where they would bring about change from within because they were more sophisticated than other architecture students – they could draw; they were articulate; they had good intellectual skills from the lectures they'd attended. They would insist upon life drawing and live-build projects. As a vehicle for change therefore, it was pretty exciting.' Some of Hugh's intake had no O-levels: lack of paper qualifications was an insuperable obstacle elsewhere. 'One of the students was a fellow of about forty. He'd been a builder in Leicester and had no qualifications whatsoever. The Foundation Course diploma for him was a passport into tertiary education – he went straight into the second year of a degree course at a School of Architecture and came out with a First Class degree. There was no stopping him. For people like that, it was so rewarding to give them a proper start and to see them fulfil their potential.'

The Institute also gave Hugh practical experience. Acting partly as a tutor and partly as the de facto clerk-of-works who oversaw the conversion of two Nash town houses overlooking Regent's Park (lately used as a prep school) to a school of architecture and craft, he got used to 'being organised and juggling different things.' While there he gave himself 'the education he had never had,' meeting craftsmen such as renowned master carver Dick Reid. Another inestimable bonus was that the administrator of the Institute was Chloë Forrester who had lately been studying History of Art at St Andrew's; Hugh married Chloë in 1995. The first of their children Harry arrived in 1999, followed by Charlotte in 2000. There were also benefits to his career. Work came to him through the contacts he made at the Institute, not least it's chairman Michael Abrahams. Indeed, he had already secured some useful projects, but at that stage had not obtained his licence to practice as an architect on his own, so he returned to Winchester Design. This had changed in line with the economic climate. In the boom years of the mid- and late-1980s it had employed around forty five people; now, in the depths of the 1990s recession, numbers had shrunk to little more than a dozen. 'I went back into the firm as an associate, working out of my spare bedroom in London and building up a portfolio of projects while continuing to teach at the same time.' By 1997 Hugh's project work was expanding rapidly so he stood back from the teaching role to focus upon his career in architectural practice.

One of the attractions of the ADAM office was the diversity of the work. This remains a characteristic. The breadth is important to Hugh. 'It makes life more interesting because every day is different. I always argue that my high-end experience has given me a design finesse that I can then apply to more commercial projects, and commercial work helps drive value in high-end commissions. We endeavour to look after our staff and to pay them properly; we want to keep them for as long as possible. By having a big office with a range of things you do, you can move people around over time to gain different experience without them going to another rival firm. Working together forms bonds, friendships and trust. It builds a strong team who are efficient and who enjoy working together. And because the members of the team are multi-skilled, if one market goes a bit quiet we can focus instead on other areas of business.'

To begin with Hugh was the firm's face in London, while his own jobs were run through the office in Winchester. After six years, he became a director. A big portfolio of country-house projects included 'an enormous Baroque palace inspired by Chatsworth' which only now is being built.

Contact with The Prince of Wales's organisations did not cease altogether. In 2003, The Prince's Foundation for the Built Environment (as the Institute had been renamed two years before) was investigating the phenomenon of pattern books, a core precept of the New Urbanism movement in the USA. Working with the Duchy of Cornwall, The Foundation commissioned Hugh to write a pattern book for Tregunnel Hill and Nansledan, the urban extensions to Newquay in Cornwall which some have referred to as Poundbury Mark 2. The pattern book analysed street patterns, building types, architectural details, materials and plants according to the local vernacular, as found in and around towns and villages on the north Cornish coast. Masterplanning has become a speciality of the office. 'There are few other firms who have the capability of doing both urban design and architecture. Urbanism firms only do urban design, they don't have the architectural expertise to build things out past planning when, without ongoing control, all too often things can go badly wrong.'

Although Hugh left his beloved Rome, he maintained a relationship with the BSR through a place on its fundraising committee. Raising money for scholarships became critical after the 2010 election when the BSR's budget was decimated and the architectural scholarships stopped. A meeting of former Rome scholars in London led to a commitment to raise £1 million. This ambition was not realised but, by dint of a crowd funding campaign led by Hugh and the personal generosity of architects whose lives had been changed by their time in Rome, enough was secured to keep the scholarship programme alive. And so it remains, through crowdfunding and other activities. As part of Hugh's oversight he joined the BSR's Fine Art Faculty responsible, among other things, for selecting the scholars.

In concert with the furniture designer Luke Hughes, Hugh also revived the Art Workers' Guild (AWG). The Guild is the cradle of the Arts and Crafts movement, founded by disciples of William Morris who wanted to establish a greater union between architecture and the building crafts. The headquarters is a Georgian town house in Queen's Square, London, the yard of which was converted into a hall at the turn of the 20th century; it's walls are lined with portraits of Past Masters that form a gallery of traditionally minded architects, artists and craftspeople from the 20th and 21st centuries. Among them is the architect Roderick Gradidge who left his home in Chiswick to the AWG; this rescued the Guild's rocky finances. 'Luke Hughes and I took it in turns to be chairman,' recalls Hugh. 'By investing half of Roddy's legacy in renovating Queen's Square we tripled the income from the building. This improved cashflow allowed us to build a website dedicated to promoting members' work. It also funded a new young secretary who could make connections with the world represented by the Guild. Membership is now increasing at a rate of ten per cent each year and the demographic profile is improving.' As though that were not enough, Hugh served as a trustee of the Georgian Group from 2003 to 2015 during a turbulent period of sometimes volcanic change. He was vice-chairman for the last three years of that term.

This synopsis of Hugh's career to date shows that it is unusual, not only in terms of the architecture produced with its emphasis on continuity based on a subtle understanding of the past, but in the multitude of challenges and building types that have been addressed. The diversity of his work will be obvious from the following pages. Hugh tackles areas of architecture that other leaders of the profession find unattractive. New housing is one example: generally, this is left to the volume house builders with baleful results – big name architects do not sully their hands. Successful housing schemes require an unusual combination of skills: few practices, for example, are able both to masterplan a project and control the design after planning permission has been obtained. Taking the broad view has become second nature. So has the imaginative unpicking of knotty problems, less to do with architecture sometimes, than planning. This can be seen in projects such as his masterplan for Holker Hall in Cumbria, where architecture became key to finding a prosperous future for the estate based upon diversifying the income derived from the repurposing of redundant buildings.

At Gunton Park in Norfolk, his proposal for The Steward's House will help the art dealer Ivor Braka realise his ambition to secure a future for the deer park. Gunton, having been rescued by the architect Kit Martin who brilliantly turned the old mansion into seventeen individual homes in the 1980s, will only be preserved as an entity if a single owner of means is there to finance and protect it. To date, Braka has been that Maecenas, painstakingly buying parcels of the ancient but much abused landscape – a total of one thousand acres – to reinstate it in its original form. Deer have been returned to the park which has become a haven of wildlife – its resurgence being all the more remarkable in a county that is, elsewhere, so intensively farmed. Mr Braka has planted a million broadleaf trees. What had been the dower house is now an uber successful pub, the Gunton Arms. This has brought high-end tourism to the area – in line with county council objectives – but removed what would otherwise be the estate's second house from private occupation. A new house of similar size is needed, in the first instance to house Mr Braka and his collections, but in the longer term to attract the sort of high-net-worth individual who will follow his example of stewardship. Appropriately the new house that Hugh has designed for this purpose, in Strawberry Hill Gothick style, is called The Steward's House. With it will go five hundred acres of parkland, with the rest of Mr Braka's holding being distributed to his other houses on the estate; the whole park in turn being administered as one unit under a properly enforced management plan. It took some time for the authorities to appreciate properly the merits of the proposal which could provide a new and innovative model for the preservation of otherwise vulnerable historic, designed landscapes whose main house has either been demolished or converted to another use.

Right: The domestic calm of the dining room at Ivy Cottage. The grandfather clock was a wedding present from his parents, while the Spanish wine jug on the windowsill was rescued by Hugh's great-grandmother's family from Buenos Aires (the only surviving artefact from a shipwreck in the Bay of Biscay).

Hugh's own domain is Ivy Cottage, in the Hampshire village of Owslebury, south of Winchester. It was originally the village forge – a long, thin early-18th century building of orangey-red brick, with a tiled roof, half-hipped at the ends. At some point in the 20th century, a conservatory had been added to the north side. Bought when the children were toddlers, there came a point – in 2014 – when they could no longer stand up in their attic bedrooms. This was also an opportunity to remove the conservatory – too hot in summer, too cold in winter – and replace it with a big kitchen. This extension shelters beneath a twin gabled roof, with walls that are half-hung with tiles. Although the new work is only a few years old, it already looks as if it has always been there and the whole building has been carefully overhauled to make it more thermally efficient. The acre of garden looks out over the Itchen valley in a perspective of daffodils, tulips and dahlias, according to season. Beyond lies open downland without another building in sight. On the Reptonian principle of borrowed landscape, it gives the impression of a much larger holding.

'I am always pleased when somebody stands in front of one of my buildings and asks what I've done,' says Hugh of the work on his home. In the following pages, readers can judge for themselves how that comment might have been made. We live in an age of clamorous individuality and self-advertisement. The antidote is Hugh, erudite where necessary but never anything but calm. Sound building materials are combined with a deep sense of place. The effect is restorative. All is right with the world.

Left: Looking through the front door of Ivy Cottage. The Gothic inner front door was designed by Hugh.

Above: The drawing room of Ivy Cottage looking through to the hall to the sitting room. Part of the existing house which Hugh renovated.

NEW HOUSES

NEW HOUSES

A STONE HOUSE OUTSIDE LONDON

The owners of this magnificent new house near Windsor like to call it a palace, and they have a point. Everything about the façades expresses grandeur. Built entirely of limestone, it has immense Corinthian porticos on both the main façades, supporting sculptural pediments (interwoven with a secondary Ionic order). The surprise of finding this noble building hiding behind the trees of the home counties lends drama to the approach. On an old site planted with a once-famous collection of azaleas and rhododendrons and numerous tall and handsome trees, the house already gives the impression of having settled into its landscape. But not all is as it seems. For the splendid outside conceals an interior made of unfinished spaces – bare rooms, since the internal divisions can be moved to suit the eventual owner.

As might be expected, the circumstances of the commission to create this triumphant set-piece – or, for the time being at least, stage set – were unusual. In 2004, Hugh was approached by the French Canadian representative of a Russian client who had recently acquired what was then half the site. On it was a 1970s house, in the manner of a Californian ranch. With it went planning permission for thirty-five thousand square feet. Although only a generation old, the existing property would be torn down and replaced. The client wanted to explore stylistic options for that building's successor. He had no specific requirements for the plan, wanting only that it should be appropriate to a house of the scale he intended. Hugh duly prepared three different schemes: the Palladian, the Arts and Crafts and, to enliven the debate, an exuberant Baroque design, surmounted by a dome. To his surprise, it was the last that the client fell for – to the extent of wanting it developed exactly as Hugh had presented it. Inevitably, stone-built Baroque architecture carries a very substantial extra cost: the plasticity of the style requires a greater volume of stone. This was of little interest to the client, who asked only, 'Will it be beautiful?' Assured that it would be, he ordered the project to proceed.

Eventually other considerations prevailed and the site, with Hugh's concept design, was put on the market. The buyers were the luxury property company Bath & Bath, owned by Tejit and Jess Bath. They announced that they intended to secure planning permission and to build the scheme as devised as faithfully as possible. Any initial scepticism that this would be done on a speculative basis has been scattered to the winds. Although the proposed dome was rejected by unimaginative planners, the scale of the house is so big that it was found possible to obtain an extra floor of sometimes top-lit rooms, around an internal courtyard, behind the deep entablature of the architrave. More land was acquired. With the various secondary buildings on what had become an estate of nearly fifty acres, the property could be offered with sixty-five thousand feet of accommodation. The main house may only have been a shell – but what a shell.

Either side of the entrance façade are deep dependencies, creating a courtyard – an effect comparable to the House in the Channel Islands (page 72). As there, the view – in this case over the park and distant woods, with no other building to be seen – is reserved until we have walked through the house, where there is the opportunity to stroll onto a broad terrace. Because the ground falls away, the garden front has an extra storey, in the form of a basement containing swimming pool and (potentially double-height) cinema. A quarry in Burgundy was chosen because they could assure the supply of the volume of stone needed over the desired building period. Not only is the whole building faced in stone but the blocks are exceptionally large. A big building requires deep courses of ashlar, as well as immense drums for the columns: too many joints would have appeared fussy – or as Hugh puts it, 'we didn't want columns looking like tubes of fruit pastels'. Indeed, with Arts and Crafts attention to detail, he ensured that the mortar in the joints was of the same colour as the stone, so that the eye sees principally the masses of which the building is made, not the grid of lines separating the blocks. For the power of this work lies in its scale. As in the Levine Building at Trinity College, Oxford, Hugh has let the beautiful materials speak for themselves, with little extraneous ornament. The structure is also based on the same principle: a concrete frame to which the self-supporting stone walls are attached. A gap between the two surfaces ensures that no water can penetrate, while the heavy mass of the building is thermally efficient.

The Corinthian capitals are of the Palladian kind, in which the acanthus leaves are more like smooth tongues of stone rather than fretted and veined in imitation of the plant from which they

---

Page 28/29: Trees and sweeping lawns provide a parkland setting for the compelling Baroque architecture of the Stone House outside London. The exterior was built speculatively by developers leaving the interior to be fitted out in the taste of a future owner.

Previous spread: The limestone Corinthian splendour of this magnificent country house belies the interior which awaits a buyer to make it a home.

Left: River gods in the pediment of the garden front, carved by Alexander Stoddart. The Corinthian order used here has stylised leaves, in the manner of Palladio.

are derived. These days computers can assist in the process of carving once a prototype has been approved, and since the end result is finished by a craftsman there is no loss in terms of the beauty of handwork – only considerable reductions in time and cost. This meant that decorative garlands to either side of the portico, modelled by the late master carver Dick Reid, could be brought within budget. Six stone factories across France were mobilised to produce this and other work. Behind the portico, at first floor level, is a Venetian window. All the windows around the building are made from stained hard wood, with fillets of gold leaf on the inner faces of the frames, in a nod to the splendours of Chatsworth. Numerous French windows on the ground floor give access to the terrace and garden.

As yet, the interior of this palatial building has something of the character of Clandon Park after the fire which gutted it. The footings of an exciting Baroque staircase can be seen in the entrance hall but the stair itself does not exist. But whereas the rooms at Clandon were largely destroyed when the flames stripped them back to the bare structure, those here are awaiting completion by the individual who will make it a home. Who will this be? The sculpture adorning the pediments at the front and back of the house leaves the question open. Created by Alexander Stoddart, it comprises four Classical river gods (leaning on their elbows, their pose suits the triangular space). They represent the Rhine, the Indus (west and east), the Hudson, and the Clyde (finance and industry). All options have been catered for in this princely dwelling.

Right: While the entrance front is only two-storey, a third storey, beneath the terrace, was gained on the garden front, due to a fall in the land. Designed to look like an orangery it contains a swimming pool whose floor can be raised by electric motors to double as a dance floor when needed.

Four doors give onto the garden from this south-facing elevation. The window frames are stained hardwood and the glazing beads have been gilded, à la Chatsworth. Behind the balustrade on the first floor is a roof terrace.

View of the as-yet unadorned interior of the wing, awaiting completion by the ultimate owner.

LOWER GROUND FLOOR

KEY
A   Cinema
B   Catering Kitchen
C   Plant Room
D   Gym
E   Pool
F   Wine Cellar

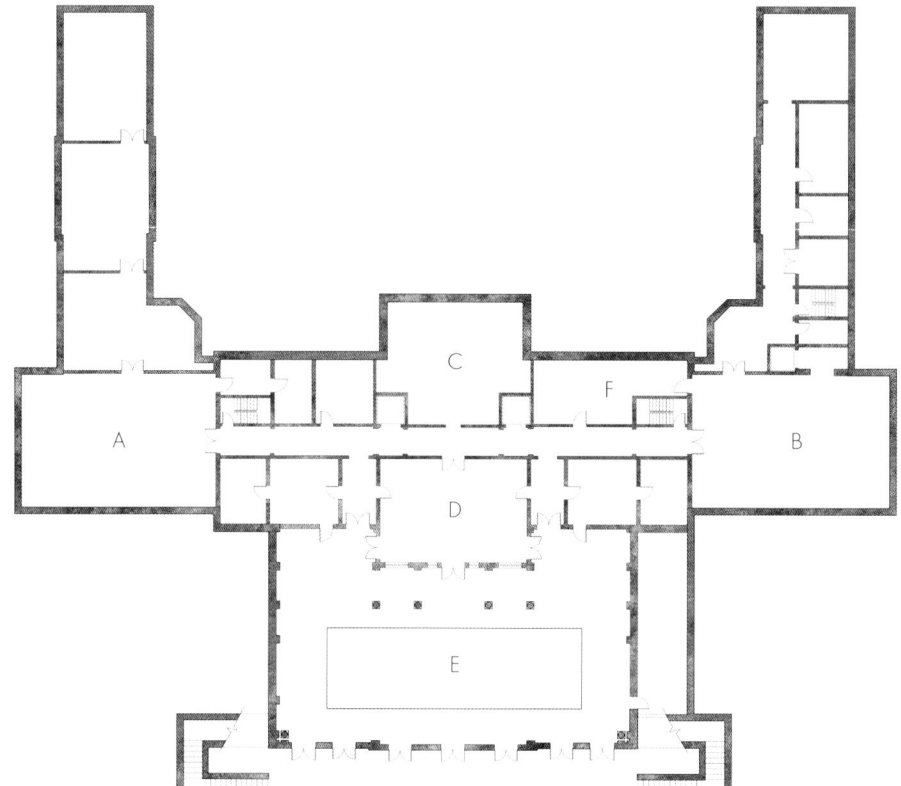

GROUND FLOOR

KEY
A   Library
B   Gallery
C   Bedroom
D   Sitting Room
E   Study/Office
F   Kitchen
G   Dining Room
H   Ball Room

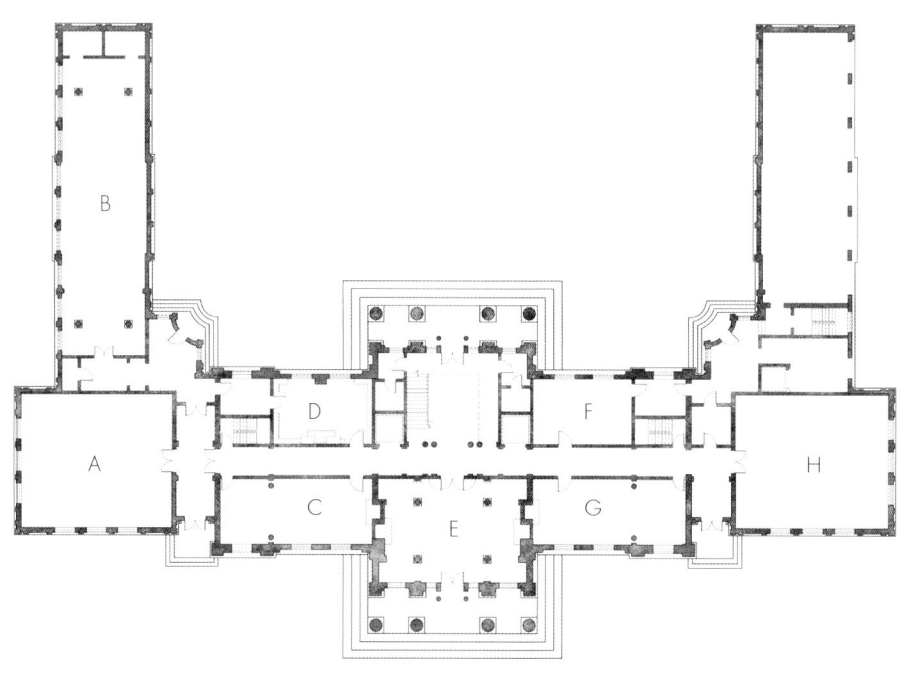

FIRST FLOOR

KEY
A   Roof Terrace
B   Master Bedroom
C   Roof Terrace

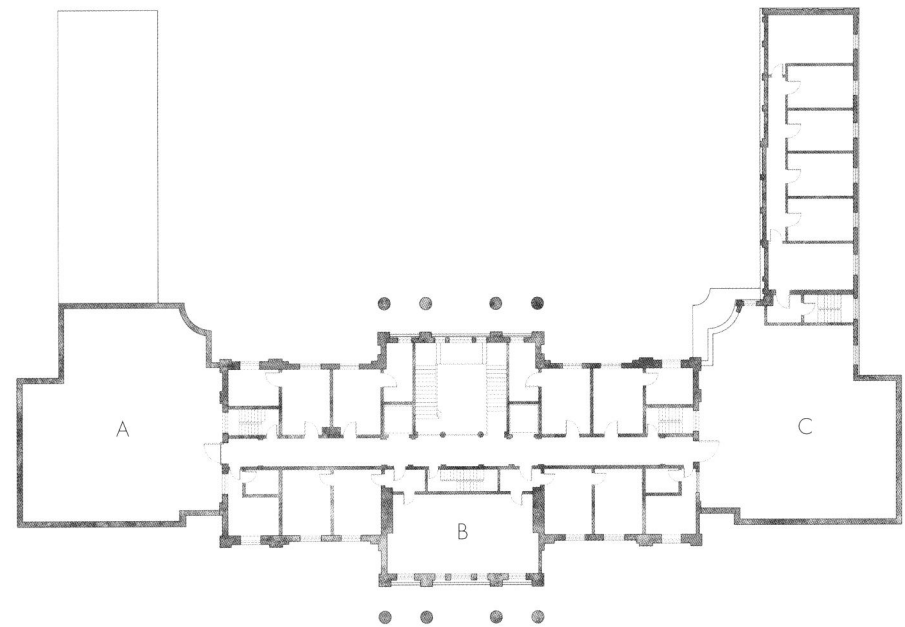

SECOND FLOOR

KEY
A   Living Room
B   Living Room
C   Bedroom
D   Bathroom

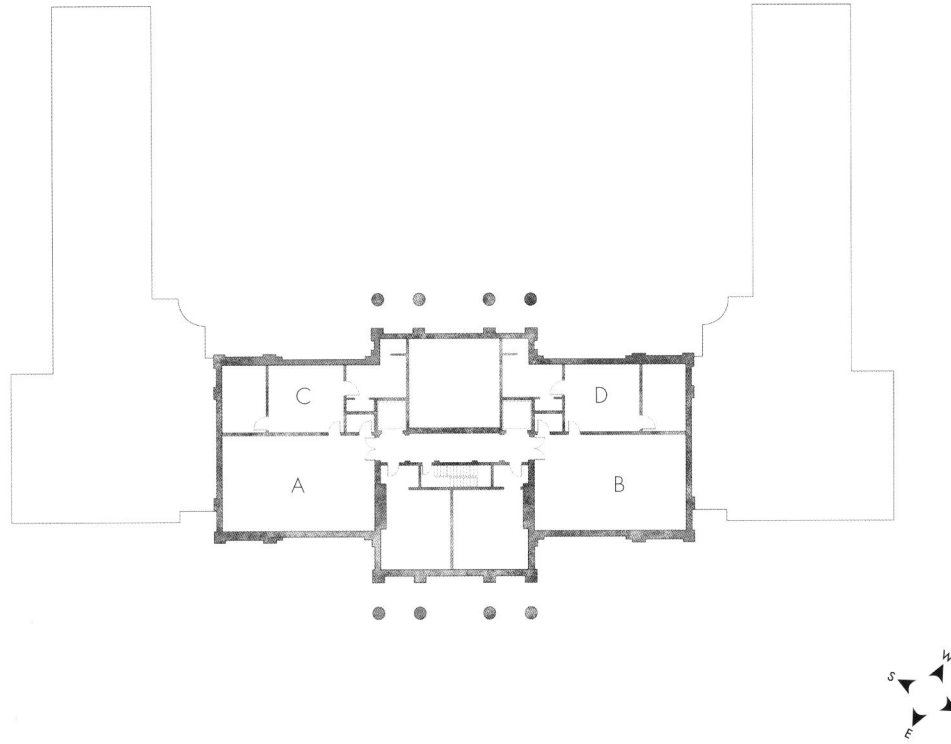

Left: View of the entrance portico on the North side of the house. Six stone factories across France were mobilised to produce the stone from which the house is built. The decorative garlands to either side of the portico were originally modelled by Dick Reid and reproduced using computer-assisted technology.

Right: A row of four Corinthian column capitals beneath the portico. The stylised leaves worked into their design were carefully chosen to complement the grand scale of the building.

Balustrade railing, made from French Burgundy limestone. Details that are conceived by an artist and finished by hand become considerably cheaper when the intervening stage is executed by modern technology.

Detail of the blind arcade from a service wing.

The garland was designed by Dick Reid: drawn, modelled in clay, plaster cast, then carved by computer-aided technology.

NEW HOUSES

BEAR ASH
BERKSHIRE

Bear Ash, near Reading, is a triumph of collaboration between Hugh as architect and Michael Balston, assisted by Marie-Louise Agius, as landscape architect. The house replaces one of many dates and little architectural quality, among whose shortcomings was a failure to take adequate advantage of the site. Major earth works created a raised shoulder of ground in front of the new building, with an enlarged lake, its edges softened by rushes, on the other side. A walled garden was an essential requirement of the client and stands on the higher ground. Below it, the house is reached by a courtyard surrounded by walls of rosy brick, given sparkle by the creamy mortar of their joints.

With a front of five bays and a central pediment, Bear Ash reads as a villa. Against walls of warm Bath Stone are accents in Moleanos Stone, a hard, pale grey limestone from Portugal: an advantage of this stone is that pediment and string course do not need to be protected from weathering by an obtrusive coping of lead. Although Bear Ash is not an especially large country house, Hugh nevertheless made the most of its potential for drama by withholding the 'big reveal' of the view to the lake until guests are inside the house. The entrance courtyard gives a feeling of enclosure; only from the hall or, if the internal doors are closed, the drawing room which is on axis with it, does the landscape first become visible.

Understandably, the client wanted as many windows as possible. On the garden front, Hugh met this design challenge by colonnades to either side of the central three bays – sash windows going down to the ground are separated only by pilasters. This, though, is not only a house to look out of but to gaze back at, its image serenely reflected in the lake. As a heron flaps slowly overhead, the house seems at one with its surroundings. While obviously belonging to the Classical tradition, Bear Ash is not overladen with ornament. As Hugh comments, 'smaller houses, they look much more dignified if they've not got too much make-up on them. Good materials with sound construction and well-proportioned windows are all that's needed.'

Previous spread: South front of Bear Ash in Berkshire. The wall stone is Bath Stone from Somerset. All the architectural detail protecting the stone is Moleanos limestone which is sufficiently hard not to require an unsightly lead flashing.

Left: The Doric entrance porch made of Moleanos limestone.

Above: The brick wall defines the entrance court but also acts as a retaining wall. The roof of the house is made from Welsh slate.

LOWER GROUND FLOOR

KEY
A   Playroom
B   Plant Room
C   Games Room
D   Utility
E   Cellar
F   Gym
G   Snug
H   Changing

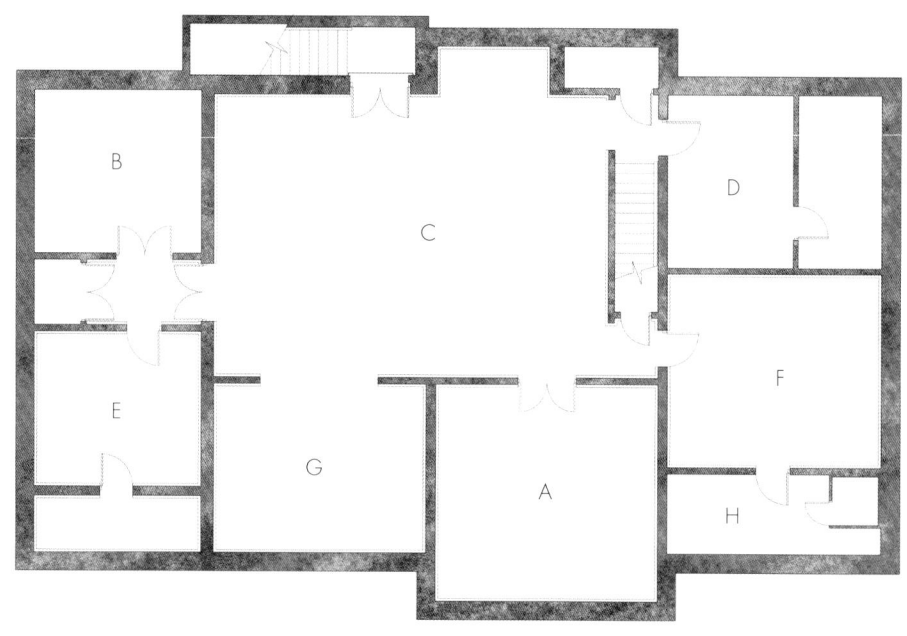

GROUND FLOOR

KEY
A   Guest WC
B   Coats
C   Hall
D   Study
E   Library
F   Drawing Room
G   Kitchen
H   Morning Room

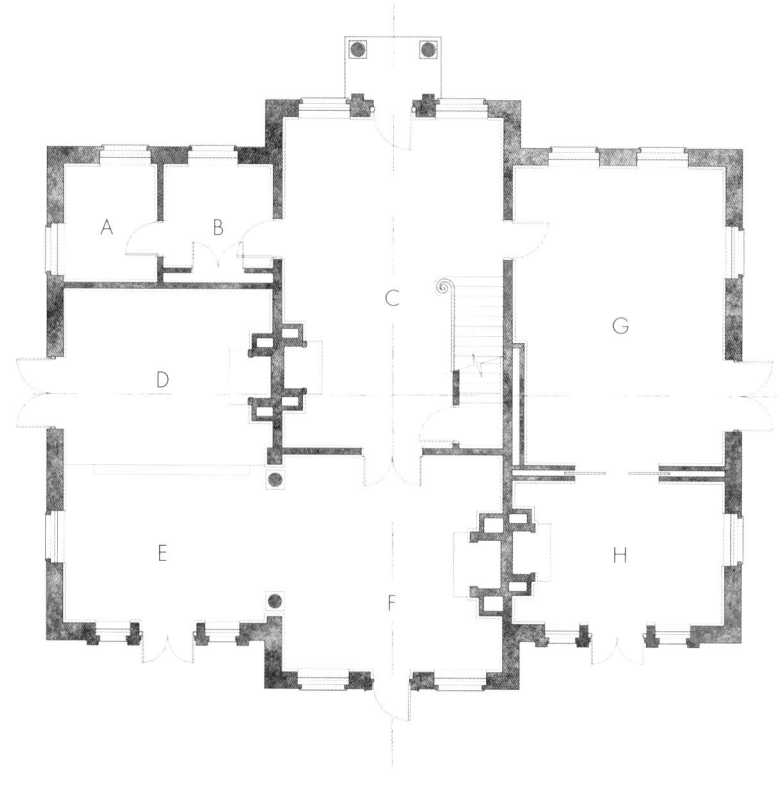

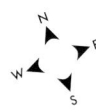

FIRST FLOOR

KEY
A   Bedroom
B   Dressing Room
C   Bedroom
D   Bedroom
E   Bedroom
F   En-suite

ATTIC

KEY
A   Storage
B   Storage
C   Storage
D   Storage

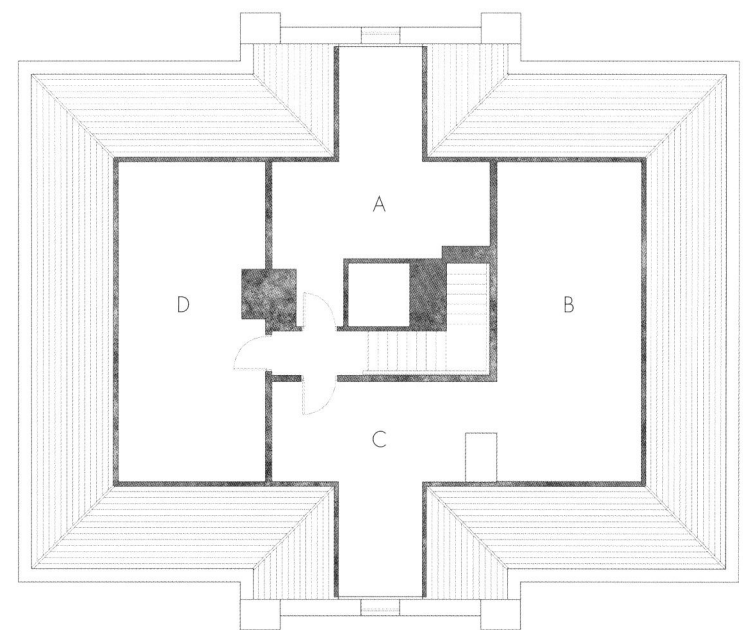

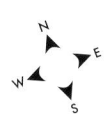

The plan is designed for flexibility. There is no dining room as such. The staircase wraps around the walls of the entrance hall. Pocket doors can be pulled out of the walls, as desired, to separate the kitchen-cum-dining room from the morning room, with its view east over the landscape. After completion, another set of pocket doors was introduced to separate the study from the library, which in turn communicates with the drawing room. While apparently a villa, Bear Ash has more living space than would be found in a Georgian equivalent, due to the extra floor of family rooms to be found in the basement (an 18th-century architect might have used it for the servants' rooms that are not needed today). This satisfied the planners, who were otherwise opposed to a new house of significantly greater volume than the previous building. Excavation enabled the provision of tall ceiling heights. Here are gym, cinema and space for children's parties. More accommodation is provided in the attic, complete with oeil-de-boeuf window for a final view of the lake.

Left: The large kitchen windows overlooking the garden bathe the room in light.

Above: The pocket doors provide a glimpse of the morning room (H on the plan).

Page 48/49: South front overlooking the garden designed by Marie-Louise Agius of Balston Agius. To maximise the window space within the Classical context, Hugh took inspiration from the banked windows used in the Regency: windows go down to the floor and are separated by Doric pilasters.

Above: The drawing room, with Doric screen separating the sitting area from that used as a library and study (E on the plan).

Right: Another view of the drawing room, looking out into the garden. Furniture has been arranged around the columns in the room, creating the sense of different areas without losing space.

NEW HOUSES

STANTON FARM
WILTSHIRE

Bungalow-eating was a term coined by the late Dr Giles Worsley to describe the effacement of an ugly building with a beautiful one, often Classical. In its purest form, a 1960s bungalow was hidden behind better proportioned façades; but by extension it has been taken to mean the replacement of any architectural horror with a handsome new structure built of traditional materials, with a front door in the right place and a happy relationship with its setting. This is what happened at Stanton Farm in Wiltshire's Pewsey Vale; the Vale makes up a large part of the North Wessex Downs Area of Outstanding Natural Beauty and the Pewsey White Horse, cut into a hillside of the Downs, can be seen from the grounds. Like so many other country house projects, the result depended on correctly finessing the planning system. In this, Hugh's experience paid dividends.

Where there had once been, if not a bungalow, at least an impoverished farmhouse of many dates, with no two matching windows and a visual litter of silage clamps, muck heaps, piles of old tyres and burnt out cars, now stands a dignified country house in the Regency manner. The transformation is complete. The new house does not merely occupy the footprint of the old one but is significantly larger than what went before.

The owner had met Hugh through a building in Savile Row where they once both had offices; the fact that they both travelled to work on a scooter formed a bond. From being a friend, he also became a client. The old house had been, says the owner, all but uninhabitable when he bought it in 2003; there were no showers and the bath could only be turned on using a monkey-wrench. This led him to knock on Hugh's Savile Row door and before long a scheme had been sketched, literally on the back of an A4 envelope. But there remained the difficulty of obtaining planning consent. To begin with, the owner and his wife would have been happy with a three bay house. Knowing, however, that difficulties might arise with the planners, Hugh proposed submitting a bigger scheme: a five-bay house which could be reduced if necessary. To everyone's surprise, this submission was approved unconditionally. This may have caused some head-scratching over the means to fund the project, but the owners soon realised that the larger house suited them better and they were particularly grateful to have it once they had started a family. The design, though elegant, is not elaborate. Using a local contractor, the owner was able to build it for the price per square foot of a house from Barratt Homes.

Previous spread: South elevation of Stanton Farm in Wiltshire. A Regency-inspired design, with large windows, bracketed eves and a simple hooded porch.

Left: The entrance front of this beautifully proportioned but simple house stands behind a paddock. Quoins give emphasis to the central bay. There is a Doric porch.

Above: A view of the farm house showing the barns visible on both sides. The way in which the house sits between the barns is very much in the Palladian manner.

Brick outbuildings to either side of the house were made into garages. The house itself was replaced with a building of rendered façades and a low-pitched slate roof. The Regency look of the roof was augmented by brackets under the eaves. This, the owner believes, is one of three small elements that transform the design from boring rectangle into a building of architectural interest. The other two are, on the north side, the entrance porch and, on the south side, a slight break forward of the central section – just enough to give variety without disturbing the line of the eaves. When the house came to be sold following a divorce, prospective buyers invariably commented on the excellent flow, from a well-appointed boot room in the outbuildings via a light link passage to the kitchen (the grand front door was rarely used).

Simplicity is all at Stanton Farm; it is a sterling vindication of Hugh's mantra that 'New Classical Design doesn't have to be complicated or ornate – elegance is achieved through the right materials and proportions.' Simplicity, though, requires discipline and it is not every architect who can achieve it. The result is a building that, although larger than the original, adds to the charm of the magical countryside in which it sits. With 300 acres of farmland and a terrace designed by the landscape architect Michael Balston, it forms what must surely be many people's ideal of a country house for the 21st century.

Above: Stanton Farm in its setting of meadow and trees. There is a pleasant contrast between the brick of the barns and the stucco of the main house.

GROUND FLOOR

KEY
A   Dining Room
B   Drawing Room
C   Entrance Hall
D   Sitting Room
E   Playroom
F   Kitchen
G   Garage
H   Farm Office
I   Boot Room

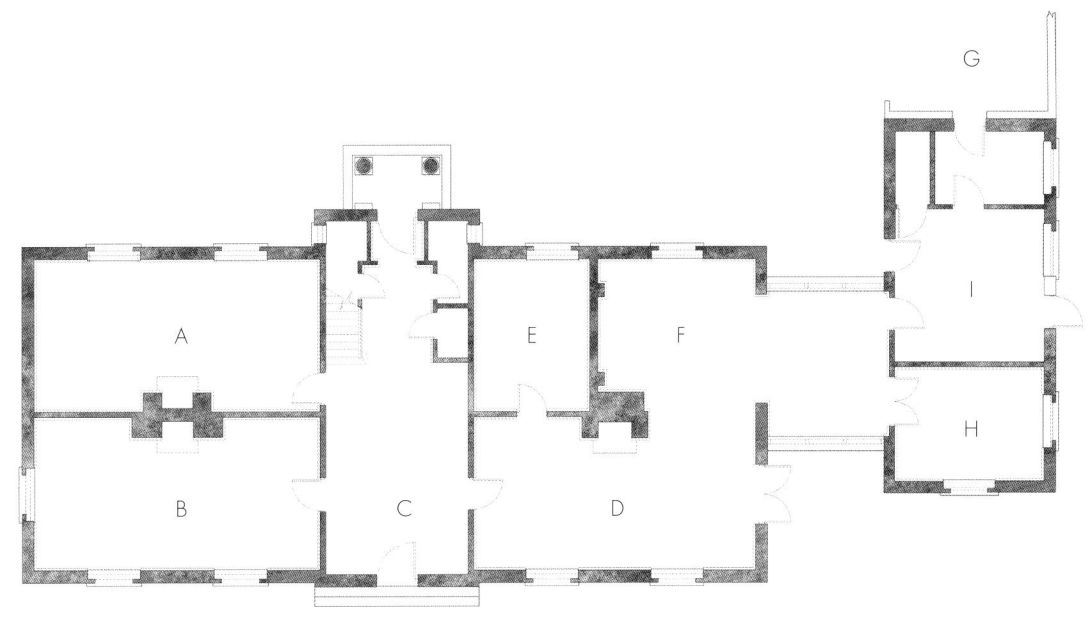

FIRST FLOOR

KEY
A   Bedroom
B   Bedroom
C   Bedroom
D   Dressing Room
E   Bedroom
F   Bedroom

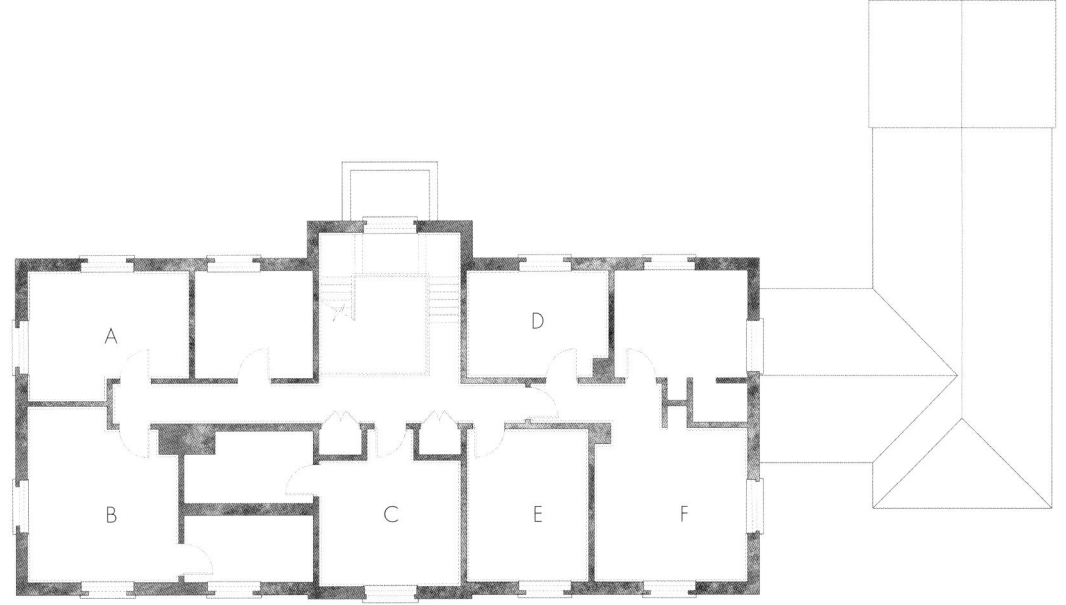

NEW HOUSES

PEMBROKE HOUSE
PARADISE ISLAND, BAHAMAS

In 1994, the late Sol Kerzner, famous for the Sun City resort in South Africa, bought Wild Pig Island off Nassau in the Bahamas and renamed it Paradise Island. Next to what was then called the One and Only Ocean Club, used as a location in the film Casino Royale, he created an exclusive residential enclave on the site of the old airport and golf course. John and Abby Barroll Brown bought lot number one.

Previous spread: Entrance porch of Pembroke House. Strong colours are needed to withstand the Caribbean sun.

Left: The double-cube high entrance hall: simple, elegant proportions inspired by Palladio. Mahogany is used for the staircase and throughout the house, as the only wood capable of resisting both the salt in the air and termites.

John Barroll Brown was introduced to Hugh through his investment in London Bridge City, the ultra-suave office development in London designed by Foster and Partners. Mr Barroll Brown told Ken Shuttleworth, one of the partners in Foster, that he wanted to build a 'very colonial, very traditional' house in the Bahamas and asked for a recommendation. Despite the difference in the architectural approach of their respective practices, Mr Shuttleworth's choice fell upon Hugh. One glance is enough to show it is in the Caribbean: only strong colours – the house is painted egg-yolk yellow – will stand up to the intense sunlight; walls painted white can be uncomfortable on the eyes because of the glare. There was also a design code – 'a file the size of a dictionary,' remembers Abby Barroll Brown – to comply with. But in form and plan, the house is also the product of Hugh's other experience of warm-weather regions. His time in Rome had shown him that rooms with tall ceilings and cross ventilation were likely to stay cool. The Classical summer schools he had taught in Virginia introduced him to porches and other indoor-outdoor spaces.

In the manner of Hugh's hero Lutyens, this house keeps visitors guessing; on first arrival, they are denied the spectacular view of the sea that lies on the other side of the property (it would be an idea he would later take with him to the Channel Islands). The entrance front is flanked, in Palladian style, by dependencies. (There are tanks underneath them for rainwater storage.) The whole of the back elevation, however, is a two-storey Doric porch, onto which it is possible to stroll from either the living rooms or the bedroom floor. This is where much of the life of the house would take place. There are chimneys and therefore fireplaces. Why are they needed, the client was once asked. 'For Father Christmas, of course,' came the reply.

Inside, the rooms are arranged around a central staircase – an example of the favourite 'doughnut plan' – on an eighteen foot grid. This module controls the volumes: for example, rooms may be eighteen foot square with a twelve foot ceiling, or thirty-six foot long and eighteen foot wide – in each case, creating a satisfying 3:2 ratio. Mahogany is used throughout, being the only wood that will withstand the sun, salt spray and termites. All the joinery was made on the island. Local supervision was provided by the Bahamian architects Robert Whittingham Design Consultants.

Above: View from the courtyard garden to the double-height portico. Two versions of the Doric order are used, Renaissance on the ground floor and an Antique one above – a chronological inversion which reflects the happy-go-lucky nature of Bahamian life. There are pergolas in front of the dependencies to either side.

Mrs Barroll Brown sums it up by saying: 'We wanted it to be a nice commodious but comfortable house, which it was. It was a sort of country house, but in a beachside position on the island.' There would be none of the big heavy curtains that you would find in a typical English country house. 'I wanted it to have those traditional feels without feeling heavy. I had this vision of opening the doors and having the wind blow my linen curtains open. And it was all of those things.' The look was achieved with the help of the interior designer Monique Gibson.

In the course of the project, Pembroke House changed from being purely a holiday house into one that the family would live in all year round. This affected the planning of the upstairs rooms: master bedroom and nursery were made part of one unit so that, with her husband frequently travelling, Mrs Barroll Brown would not have to go onto the hallway if the children needed her during the night. 'I was sort of enclosed and I felt very safe.'

The only drawback to Pembroke House as a family home was its popularity. 'Never build a house in the Bahamas and then casually extend invites to people,' says Mrs Barroll Brown, 'because at one point I felt like I was running a small boutique hotel. We had check in and check out as different groups came and went. This meant changing the beds over and getting everything ready. But we used the dining room every night and it was beautiful.'

As the children got older, the Barroll Browns decided to relocate to the UK. But Pembroke House still has a warm place in their hearts.

Right: The first-floor verandah runs around the building providing outside space for the bedrooms. Paired columns help the house look more vertical.

View looking through into the drawing room. Internal fan lights keep the room bright and airy.

LIVING TRADITION

Dining room, with mahogany fittings.

Master bathroom. The door gives onto a veranda.

Suggestion of the glorious ocean views that are to be had from the first floor verandas.

NEW HOUSES

A HOUSE IN THE CHANNEL ISLANDS

You know that something special is happening at this house as soon as you pass the restored farm buildings at the entrance. The drive, once tarmac, is made from granite setts imported from Paris which provide an elegant, variegated surface with simple drains at the sides. The house is hidden from view until the drive turns towards it revealing a five-bay composition with a central pediment. There are dependencies to either side enclosing a courtyard. All is built from a lightly-figured, honey-coloured limestone, speckled with brownish tints of iron oxide, from Cadeby in Derbyshire: a stone that is tough enough to withstand the salt-laden storm winds that lash it in winter. Details are cut from Moleanos Stone, a hard, pale grey limestone similar in appearance to Portland Stone but harder – an advantage being that pediment and string course do not need to be protected from weathering by an obtrusive coping of lead. The quality of the ashlar indicates a superb standard of finish, and this is indeed apparent throughout the house.

The clients wanted there to be 'a sense of arrival.' But the entrance, in the manner of the great architectural magician, Hugh's hero Sir Edwin Lutyens, does not disclose its true nature at first glance. Even the entrance hall, although spectacular in the patterned stonework of the floor and the two cantilevered staircases that rise up to either side, withholds the real point of the house. This is the view, which explodes on the eye when you walk around to the enfilade on the south side. You can hardly stop yourself from walking out onto the broad terrace to say 'wow'.

There are rocks, capes, islets and the glistening sea, familiar from Impressionist paintings because Renoir came here. Difficult to access, the little grey-sand beaches are two of the best on Guernsey but generally deserted. The terrace is designed to take scores of guests, for this is a party house par excellence. To one side is a South African garden planted in blocks of exuberant colour. As yet you are unaware of the second 'big reveal', and that is the basement storey, which, in true iceberg style, is double the size of the house above. The basement is about fitness and leisure. It is where you will find the swimming pool, the gym, the sauna, the cinema, and spaces for the owners' record collection and wine. Conventionally, people speak of wine cellars but the term is hardly appropriate here; the bottles – many thousands of them – are stored in what look like library cases, arranged in a Borromini-esque false perspective of diminishing size. The basement is faced in dark grey granite from Spain which resembles the native Guernsey blue, the seam for which is temporarily exhausted. The surface of the stone has been hammered by hand to create a dimpled texture in a technique known as dolly pointing. From the sea, the dark granite, contrasting with the light limestone of the upper floors, reads as part of the landscape; sailors will notice only the balustrades of the terrace and a giant Ionic order. The house appears to be two storeys rather than three.

Fortunately, the clients have a wide experience of building projects and were not daunted by the obstacles encountered in their pursuit of their dream home. These included a change of architect: their original choice succeeded in achieving planning permission for a large country house – itself no mean feat on the island – but it was largely underground, hence the importance of the basement to the finished project (Hugh's project was negotiated from the existing consent). The prospect of subterranean living did not satisfy the clients' desire for 'spacious, grand rooms overlooking the sea.' They liked Palladian proportions and wanted a house that would not hide from the view, without dominating it. They wanted 'a very large bedroom from which we could look at the sea, with our own studies and dressing rooms to either side. Effectively we have got a big bedroom with two office areas next to it, which works well.' The top floor is entirely occupied by these private spaces. The ground floor is for entertaining. Doors onto the terrace can be flung open on a fine day. Doors that either fold back into the panelling or disappear completely into pockets in the wall enable guests to flow from one room to another. The impressive family kitchen is planned around a black granite table top weighing eight hundred pounds. One of the wings of the dependencies contains a catering kitchen. The glamour of the butlers' pantries is beyond anything known by Jeeves.

Throughout the house, the interior designer John Minshaw's finishes are figured woods and sumptuous stones – natural, but of the most sumptuous kind and executed with a precision of craftsmanship that aspires to the divine. Much of these luxury surfaces were made in Norfolk where they could be crafted to a level that would not have been possible on site. To the clients, the result is 'uplifting'. They find that 'each and every room has its own presence. They all look right for what they do.' The accommodation for guests has been as carefully considered as that of the rest of the house. Here, the clients'

Previous spread: The rocky beach rises to a lawn: a spectacular setting for this house in the Channel Islands.

Left: Entrance elevation. The house is flanked by dependencies in the Palladian manner.

professional experience of hotels has come into play. The guests' staircase does not intersect with that of the owners. Bedrooms have been subjected to a high level of analysis as regards the wants of those staying in them. 'We'd like to think that if the Four Seasons gave you a guest suite like that, you'd be happy.' On behalf of all their lucky guests I'd like to say that I would.

Right: The falling site made it possible to introduce a basement (for swimming pool, spa suite and other facilities) with a broad terrace above it. The grey granite comes from Spain, a close fit to local stones that can no longer be obtained. The rest of the house is built from Cadeby limestone from Derbyshire, with details picked out in hard Moleanos limestone from Portugal.

Above: The pool with light flooding through the surrounding windows, looking out onto the garden.

Right: Decorator John Minshaw's sketch for the library, with its dramatic lantern centerpiece.

Following spread: The side elevation rises above a South African garden.

RESTORATION

RESTORATION

CHETTLE HOUSE
DORSET

Chettle House near Blandford Forum is regarded by *The Buildings of England* as the plum among Dorset's early-18th-century country houses. This is not because of its size. Built by the gentleman architect Thomas Archer, who had a lucrative court appointment to keep the wolf from the door, it is rich in Baroque architecture – Archer must have studied Borromini while on his Grand Tour in Italy – but relatively compact. The corners of Chettle's façade are curved, as though it were a piece of sculpture as much as a building. Among the many idiosyncratic touches is a uniquely personal interpretation of the Corinthian Order. But by 2015, when it was bought by the present owners Tim and Rosamond Sweet-Escott, this nationally important building had fallen on hard times. The interior had been divided into seven flats after the Second World War to provide income, but upkeep became an increasing struggle. Water seeped through the patched roof.

Page 82/83: Chettle House, in Dorset. West elevation from the lime avenue in the park.

Previous spread: The East front, with reflecting pool by Pip Morrison. Hugh restored Chettle's brickwork and stonework, and replaced the lead.

Left: South elevation of Chettle. The house was reduced by a storey in the 19th century due to rot, then built up again, with Hamstone dressings, in the Edwardian period. The original stone was Chilmark green sandstone. The circular pool survives from a previous phase of the garden.

Hugh's task was to reinvent Chettle as somewhere untouched by time. This involved a major campaign of works. All the internal partitions and unsightly bathrooms had to go; false floors in the basement were removed; saturated walls given the chance to dry out, at the rate of an inch a month. The entire place was encased in scaffolding while the roof was restored with Welsh slate and thirty-five tons of lead. Instead of only two outlets to allow water to drain from the gutters, there are now eight. Every chimney has been lined with pumice, a more practical solution than the usual steel liners although regular holes had to be made in the walls to install it. A tent was set up for the stonemasons to work in. Diggers crawled over the garden excavating ponds and reshaping the grounds. And yet the end result gives a serene impression of continuity. Who would guess from looking at the sash windows, their crown glass sparkling in the sun, that every one of them had been taken out and remade? Authentically wavy glass was used to replace broken panes.

Originally, Chettle's roofline was different. Behind a flamboyantly broken pediment, somewhat like that which survives on Archer's church of St John's Smith Square in London, was an extra bedroom floor. The owners had no appetite to recreate this feature which would have made the house too big. They were, however, able to create three handsome attic rooms for their children, now grown up, with access to the hidden terrace on the roof. On a sunny day there can be nowhere better to while away the afternoon than this eyrie, with its view over a new Baroque landscape inspired by fragments of the original.

Doing anything to a Grade 1 listed house is not for the faint-hearted: owners who have nothing but the best intentions can become so disillusioned by the demands of the planning system that they wish they had never started. This has not been the case at Chettle. Perhaps there were minor skirmishes: over, for example, an attempt to protect a moulding which, when part of it was removed, was found to have a barcode on the back (evidently it was not quite so old as had been thought). But for the most part harmony reigned, decisions were made quickly and the building work proceeded to time. From the moment that the builders got on site, the job took barely two years to complete. Much of this can be put down to Hugh's collaborative approach developed by his experience as a senior figure in the Georgian Group. By inviting the planners and historic buildings officers to come to the house and discuss contentious issues on site – with a builder on hand to add a practical commentary – a consensus could generally be obtained there and then. It was evident that architect and owners intended to do their very best for the house. Personal knowledge of the individuals concerned gave the local authority confidence. The clients even succeeded in obtaining consent for the live-in kitchen which, for them, really makes the house work despite the breach that had to be made in an original wall. (But as Hugh could demonstrate, the history of the wall had, at various times, already been compromised.) The clients knew they would be on the same wave length as their decorator, Ben Pentreath, when they asked for orange walls: Ben was able to show them a photograph of his own kitchen at Littlebredy which has – orange walls.

Although Chettle was altered during a restoration of 1846 and another in 1910, it retains the main elements of its plan. On the eastern front is a rectangular entrance hall with a central axis through to the garden. A wooden staircase rises on two sides of this hall meeting on a gallery that crosses a third side. The exact form of the original stair is uncertain – another flight may have returned to the entrance front. However, it was decided that the stair as we have it was sufficiently dramatic to keep as it was; where necessary, the carpentry was subtly underpinned. One of the glories of Chettle is the light, which here floods through two banks of tall, round-headed windows, reminiscent of those in the hall at Blenheim. To either side, enfilades have been opened up at first-floor level.

Outside, the garden historian Kate Felus identified some banks that must have belonged to the Baroque garden; they were part of a scheme that included two squares of wilderness known as the rookeries. Other features could only be guessed at, or intuited from remains of historical planting. Avenues have been reinforced. A basin to reflect the house has been dug. Overgrown clumps of laurel and scrub were cut down to reveal the pretty church, now itself a delightful landscape feature, and open views from and to the house; a claire-voie has been erected at the end of the lawn on the garden front. All the ironwork around Chettle has been painted blue.

To one side is a kitchen garden and next to it a swimming pool. This is served by a Palladian pool house whose arched central motif is decorated with panels of cubed flint. Where would the garage go? There were no available stables or other outbuildings near the house since they had been sold away from the estate by previous owners. While a garage near the house was felt to be essential for the transfer of groceries and other impedimenta from car boot to kitchen, the planners were adamant that it would mar the external appearance of the house. In the end it was decided that the garage should be partially sunk underground. It was, says Tom Sweet-Escott with the generosity of spirit which has somehow translated itself into a happy result, the 'perfect solution. I'm glad that the planners pushed back against earlier ideas.'

Right: This aerial view of Chettle shows the 'secret' room that has been created on the roof. The trees hint at a Baroque landscape which included a rookery and bowling green.

Previous spread: The entrance hall is mainly by the Georgian architect Thomas Archer. During the restoration, the staircase was strengthened with a flitch beam, in the manner of the original work.

Left: The stairwell looking east, with light bouncing through the banks of windows.

Right: Door into the new kitchen from the stairwell.

RESTORATION

Previous spread: The kitchen. Hugh obtained permission to remove a wall to make a proper family kitchen on the ground floor in the main part of the house, decorated by Ben Pentreath.

Above: The drawing room was created in the 19th century. New panelling was designed by Hugh in conjunction with Ben Pentreath, to fit beneath the original cornice.

Right: Thomas Archer's most complete room at Chettle is the Stone Hall. Hugh reopened the fireplaces and introduced underfloor heating beneath the original stone slabs.

LOWER GROUND FLOOR

KEY
A   Sitting/TV Room
B   Bedroom
C   Laundry
D   Services
E   Table Tennis
F   Entrance Hall
G   Boot Room

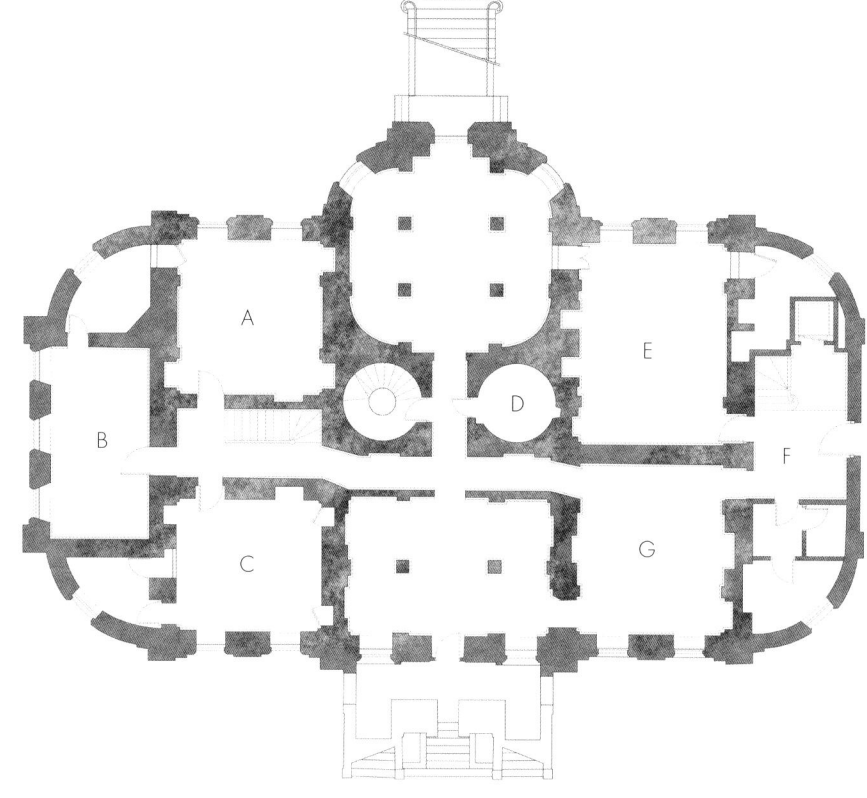

GROUND FLOOR

KEY
A   Hall
B   Dining Room
C   Pantry
D   Lift
E   Kitchen
F   Stair Hall
G   Study
H   WC
I   Drawing Room
J   WC
K   Ante Room
L   Cloak Room

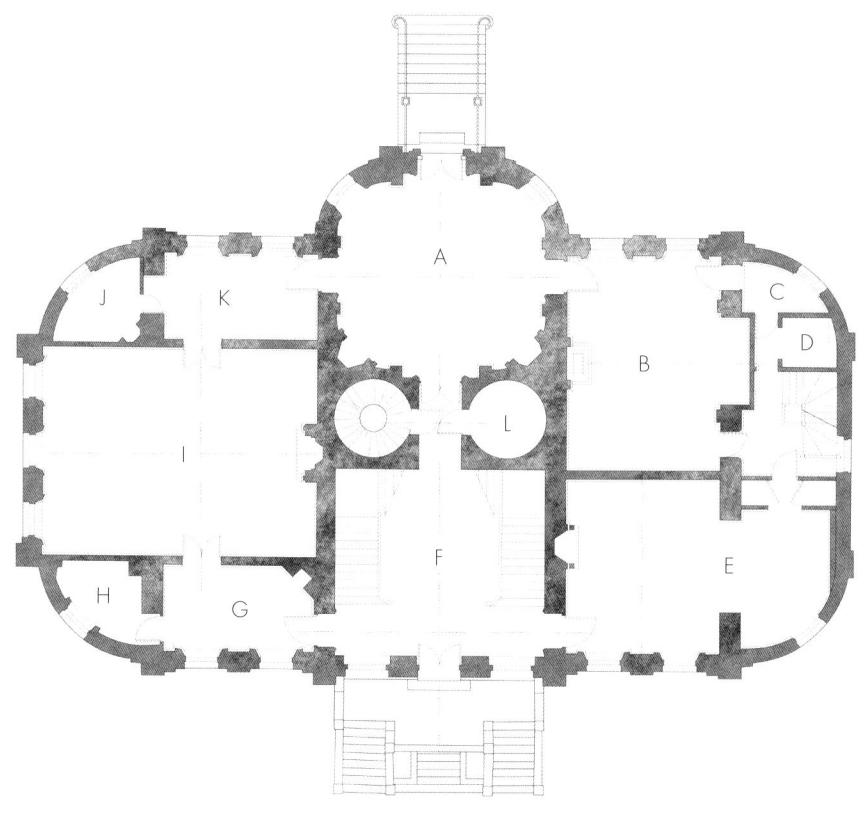

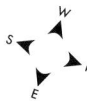

Boot room in the basement showing vaulting. A floor and various walls that had been inserted were removed to bring the space back to the original proportions and underfloor heating was added under the original flagstones.

A new bedroom in the attic.

FIRST FLOOR

KEY
A   Sitting Room
B   Bedroom
C   Bedroom
D   Bedroom
E   En-suite (Shower)
F   Bedroom

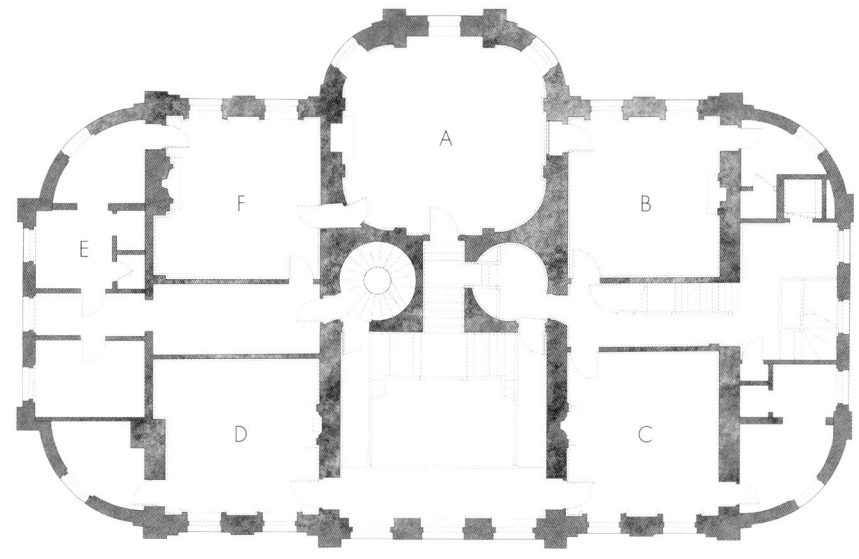

SECOND FLOOR

KEY
A   Bedroom
B   En-suite
C   Guest Bedroom
D   Bedroom

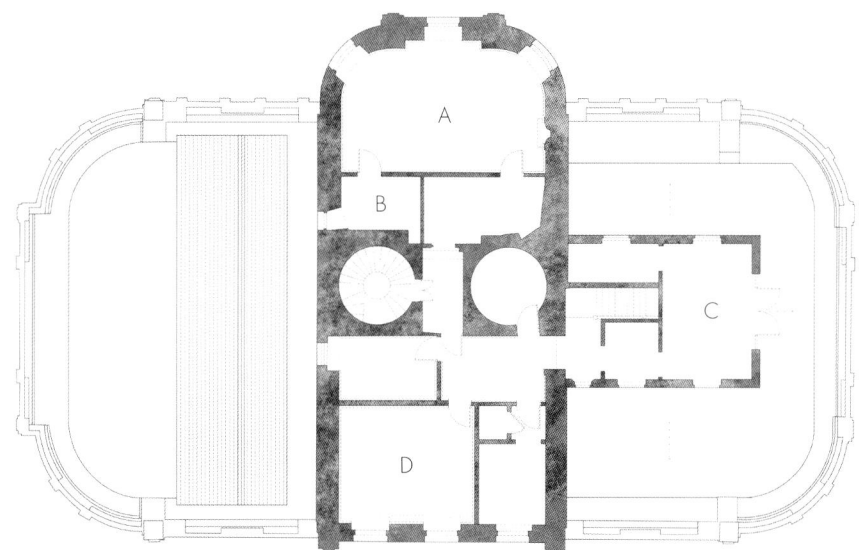

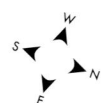

GARDEN PLAN

KEY
A   Chettle House
B   Garage
C   Pool House
D   Reflecting Pool

Following spread: The garage court, shown as B on the plan, is intended to look like a coach house.

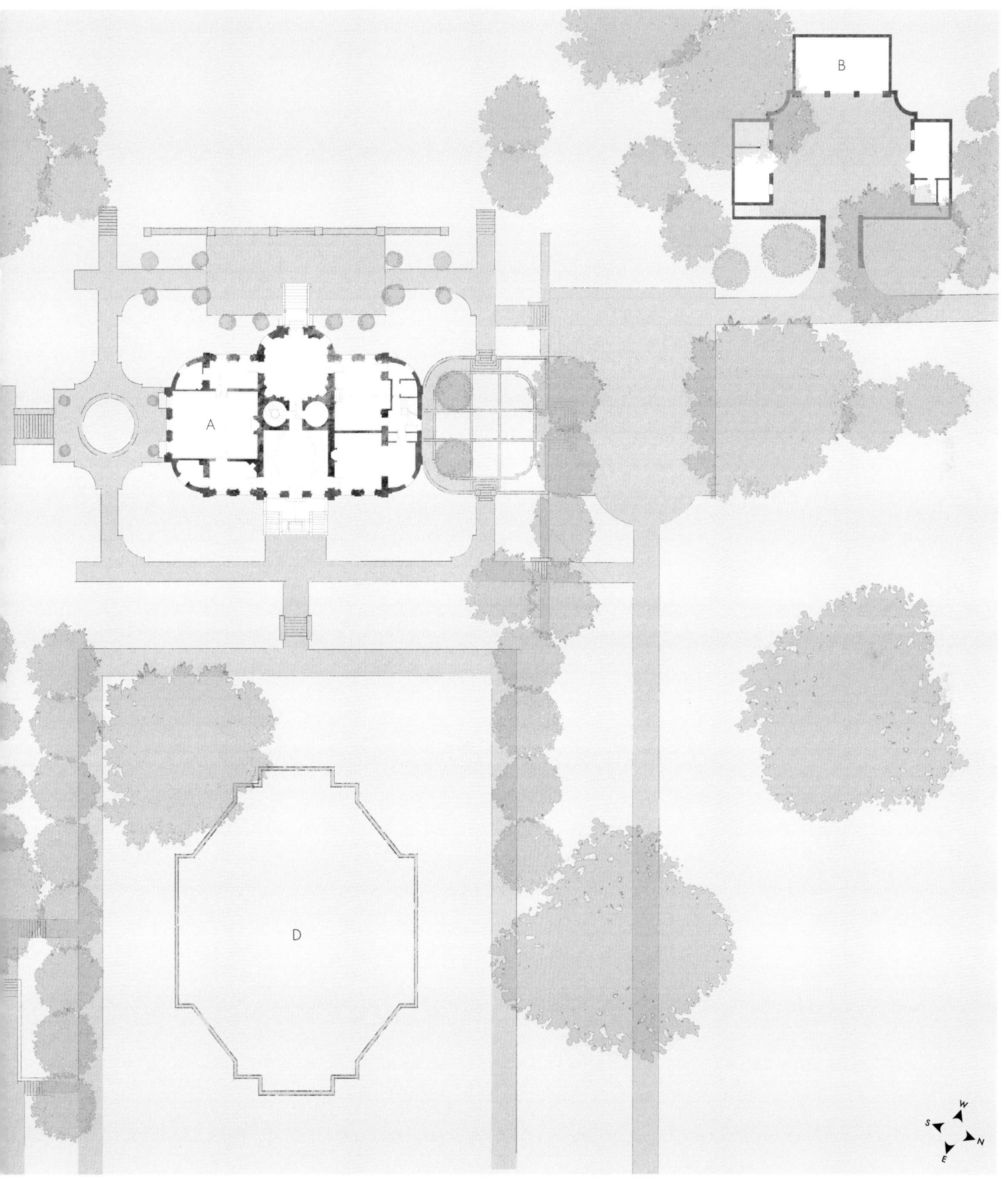

The owners keep their cars in the open arcade, recalling a Palladian *barchessa*.

Above: Chilmark Stone alternates with bands of knapped flint in the walls of the machinery store. The floor of the rectangular courtyard is laid with limestone slabs to create a pattern.

Following spread: Stone flint cube bands can be seen in the walls of the new pool house that has been created in the walled garden.

Left: Front elevation of the pool house, with a Chilmark Stone and flint banded central bay.

Above: A window of the pool house, with cubed flint decoration in the central bay.

Detail of the superb quality of the knapped flints. Iron in the flints produces flecks of gold.

RESTORATION

FAWLER MANOR
OXFORDSHIRE

The lightning bolt that struck Fawler Manor on a late August afternoon in 2012 was in some respects providential. The point of entry was the junction between the old house and its unsatisfactory Victorian front: it was largely the latter that burnt and, while the 16th-century hall was badly damaged by the water that put the fire out, the old timber-frame was saved. Once owners Philip and Christine Blackwell had recovered from the shock of seeing their home of more than twenty years reduced to a charred wreck, they welcomed it as an opportunity to rebuild, creating a house that would be much better planned, equipped and insulated than before. It is exactly the sort of project that Hugh thrives on.

There is some thought that the earliest part of Fawler Manor could belong to the 12th century, when it may have been a smoke house. Like many country buildings across England, this modest structure was enlarged and improved in the Elizabethan period when a tall brick chimney was added in 1590; this is the date that has been carved into it along with the initials RP. The result was a hall house, with cross wings to either side of the central hall. Over later centuries this early core was subdivided, and unsympathetic additions created a haphazard plan which provided no big rooms or the possibility of obtaining them. External stonework had been lost beneath pebble dash and the top floor bedrooms had nothing to protect their thin, wattle-and-daub walls from the elements. Although ancient, Fawler Manor was so flawed that the owners had already begun to contemplate building a new country house on another site to provide the spaces and comfort expected of a 21st-century dwelling. The lightning strike put an end to those plans. It was as though the gods had spoken: the Manor would be reimagined.

Today, there is no evidence of trauma by fire. Behind espaliered fruit trees, Fawler Manor's entrance front presents as sunny a face as you could find in the rosy heart of Oxfordshire. A sturdy oak porch supported by Tuscan columns shelters the front door; the cross wings step forward to either side as they always have done; and two dormers emerge from the Cotswold Stone roof. Creamy lintels and quoins made of Bath Stone contrast with the white of the lime render. Clearly this is a façade of different dates, since the windows to the west have mullions while those on the east are sashes. Few people would guess, though, that the sash windows do not date from the Georgian period: everything to the right of the front door as you look at it in the photographs is new. This has allowed for the creation of two big rooms overlooking the landscape to the south: a big kitchen – with plenty of room not just for a dining table, but also an arrangement of large sofas and armchairs around a wide fireplace – and a drawing room. The latter succeeds in being generously sized – spacious enough to absorb many large pieces of upholstered furniture as well as antiques – but unintimidating. Double doors between kitchen and drawing room can be thrown open for parties. (Beyond the garden, the hillside has been improved by the addition of a stone circle to replace a majestic tree that stood there until blown down in a gale).

The owners wanted not only a convenient plan but one that was quietly dramatic, with one space that would be open to the roof timbers. Hugh conjured this from the entrance hall which contains the main staircase. Elegantly cantilevered from the wall, the wooden stairs rise up to a ground floor gallery which is itself overlooked by the hallway of the attic floor. The attic provides bedrooms – lit by the two dormers on the entrance front, which are new – that can accommodate the Blackwells' three daughters, in their twenties and thirties, when they are there: a blessing while the whole family was together during the Covid pandemic. At first-floor level in the entrance hall, a wall opening revealed by the fire has been filled with a display of fragments of architectural detail that survived the blaze. After the height of the entrance hall, the dining room, in the old part of the house, is of intimate proportions; the low ceiling called for simple mouldings to the doorcase and cabinet work. This is in every sense a warm room, with a splendidly large fireplace and a discrete system of double glazing in wooden frames in front of the stone mullions. This double layer of glass is practically invisible, as are the argon-filled double glazing units which occupy the place of glass panes in the sash windows.

Previous spread: The south elevation of Fawler Manor with Bath Stone quoins and a new roof of Oxfordshire stone slates.

Left: Courtyard at the back door. The part facing us is old, projecting parts are new.

Aerial view of the house in its setting.

Repaired chimneys and the restored roof. Every stone slate was stripped off the fire-damaged roof and, where possible, reused on the old part of the building.

New matching Stonesfield slates were used on the new extension. The character of the roof and its chimneys were carefully maintained.

Detail of the stair hall and oak staircase.

GROUND FLOOR

KEY
A   Flower Room
B   Dining Room
C   Utility
D   Kitchen
E   Bootroom
F   Family Room
G   Drawing Room
H   Hall

FIRST FLOOR

KEY
A   Bedroom
B   Bedroom
C   Bedroom
D   Bedroom

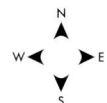

To many people, the ideal country house is one that balances opposing forces. It is domestic without being dull; grand without being chill; old without sacrificing the convenience of modern life; a work of art without being precious. Fawler Manor squares these different circles. Let us take our leave of it from the terrace that runs along the south front, looking toward a hill adorned with what might be a prehistoric stone circle, actually placed there by the Blackwells to compensate for the visual loss of a tree that blew down. Like the entrance front, this façade is a composition of Cotswold Stone roof, triangular gables and doorcases – the latter provided with a simple hood. It is not just the beauty of the materials that generates a sense of well-being and satisfaction in the viewer. Look at the roof. Only, perhaps, when you have gazed at it for some time – or had it pointed out by the architect – do you notice the different heights of the eaves. Another architect might have designed this roof with eaves all at the same level. How much more interesting it is for the eye when the levels are slightly varied. This was the Arts and Crafts way, expounded by Nathaniel Lloyd, Lutyens' client at Great Dixter, in his book *Building Craftsmanship in Brick and Tile and in Stone Slates*, 1929. To Lloyd, there was a right and a wrong way to build – and to underline the point, he labels his diagrams 'Right' and 'Wrong'. These days, it is not every architect who knows the difference.

Previous spread: View of the drawing room looking toward the kitchen. Mouldings of a Regency style were chosen since there are more on the ceilings than on the walls, thus increasing the sense of height.

Right: The kitchen with its spacious floor plan and large windows, admitting natural light.

The stair hall. The character of the roof is of an early type, without a ridge beam.

This landing is lined with bookcases to create a study alcove.

Left: Bedroom in the attic. Here again the lack of a ridge beam tells you that this is an old house.

Above: Another bedroom, showing the warm palette of the interior design.

RESTORATION

OLD RECTORY
BERKSHIRE

When flames devoured the Old Rectory at West Woodhay in Berkshire in 2011, brave firemen were able to rescue nearly all of the principal contents. As traditionally happens in the case of country-house fires, antique furniture and pictures in gilded frames found themselves unceremoniously placed on the lawns. But in dousing the flames they used over half the water in the swimming pool; the upstairs bedrooms were completely destroyed. Fortunately the fire had started on the first floor, and for a while it initially seemed that the ground floor might have survived the worst of the blaze, but before long the ceilings collapsed under the weight of water. A thick coating of sticky soot covered everything. There was no question but that the house had to be substantially rebuilt. Above all, this was a rescue mission: the Old Rectory had to be returned to its former state, complete with all the details and atmosphere which had made it a loved family home.

There was also, though, an opportunity to improve the plan, upgrade services and make better bathrooms. According to the then owner Rupert Bradstock – a serial Hugh client, he and his wife Anna have since moved to Meadow Farm on Jersey, described elsewhere in this book – the phoenix that arose from the ashes was in some respects a better bird than the one that had gone up in flames.

Hugh was a natural choice for the job since he had already done work for the Bradstocks. As Jeremy Musson describes in *The Country House Ideal: Recent Work by ADAM Architecture*, 2015, the restoration involved in part the replacement of cement render on the entrance front with lime; the installation of better proportioned windows; and adding a better porch. The porch encloses double front doors in a Doric screen: glazing to the door and panels to either side allows light into what had previously been a rather dark entrance hall. After the fire, the approach was to reinstate the structure in the spirit of the late-18th century builders, using the sorts of materials and techniques that would have been familiar to them. This meant rebuilding the roof out of oak and laying floorboards of unequal widths, as would be found in an old house. Ceilings and walls might have been replaced using plasterboard but this would not only have been historically inappropriate but subtly jarring on the aesthetic sense. Lime plaster, applied by hand to a traditional support of wooden laths, has a personality that can never be achieved by a perfectly flat wall. Admittedly it takes longer and costs more – much longer and much more – than the alternative; but the result adds greatly to the feeling of calm and mellowness that is one of the blessings of an old house. The acoustical properties meant that even the silence is different.

Previous spread: Entrance elevation of the Old Rectory, in Berkshire, showing the new Greek porch.

Left: A view of the front elevation, revealing the front porch. New lime render was applied to the walls creating a soft texture, scored in imitation of stone.

Above: After a catastrophic fire, which destroyed the Old Rectory's roof, the house was sensitively repaired.

Not every inconvenience of the old building could be ironed out: Mr Bradstock remembers that the drawing room had only one door – and the Old Rectory's listed status meant it could not have two. But the family kitchen, which occupied an early 20th century addition, was replanned. The fire also meant that the insulation could be brought up to scratch, making the house warmer in winter and cheaper to heat.

'The result,' writes Mr Musson, 'is an English classic of elegant and comfortable reserve with many fine inherited family pieces – not least the extraordinary door made for an ancestor of Mrs Bradstock by the monks of Mount Athos.' This sumptuous door with its remarkable inlay has travelled with the Bradstocks to Jersey and now opens onto one of the downstairs lavatories. 'The house has recaptured its historic qualities and been reconditioned for modern life.' Few visitors were aware of the extent of the reconstruction. To quote Mrs Bradstock, 'the house really feels just the same, only better.'

Right: The forecourt, laid with gravel. Note the sympathetic character of the new roof.

Left: A view of the kitchen from the entrance hall. The walls are finished in traditional lath and plaster, which provide a more organic finish than plasterboard. The door surrounds are late-18th century in feeling.

Above: The entrance hall, newly restored. Much of the furniture was salvaged from the original house and restored since the damage was mostly due to water.

Right: The drawing room. The fireplace in the Regency style is new. Cornices spreading onto the ceiling in the Regency manner give an impression of height. Much of the furniture was salvaged from the original house and restored.

Following spread: Entrance hall and staircase with serpentine line and mahogany handrail: all is completely new since the previous entrance hall and staircase were destroyed in the fire.

GROUND FLOOR

KEY
A   Drawing Room
B   Study
C   Dining Room
D   Family Room
E   Kitchen
F   Sitting Room
G   Entrance Hall
H   Cloak Room
I   Utility

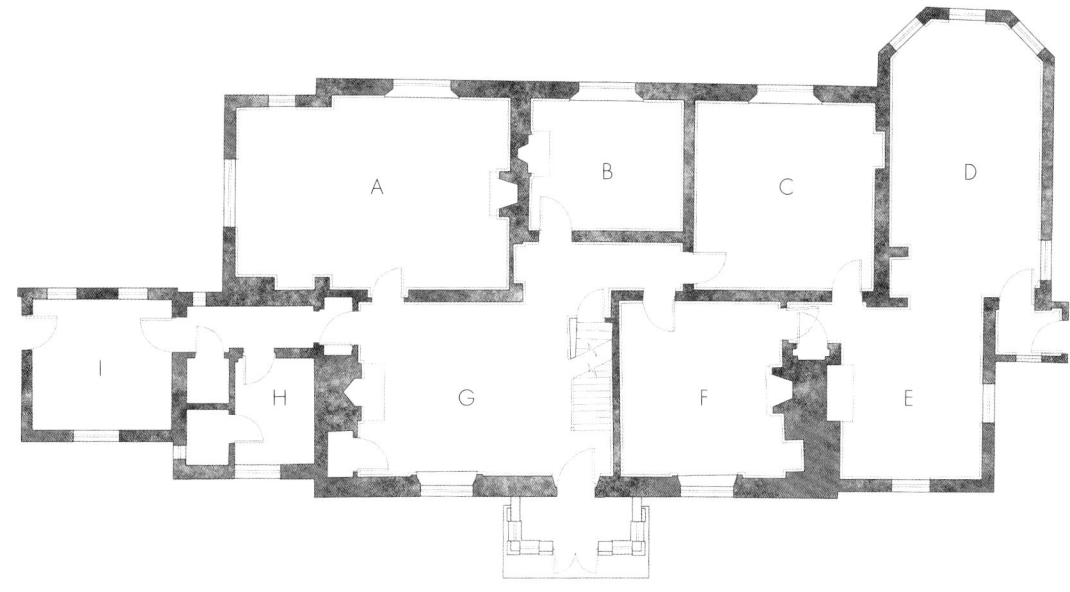

FIRST FLOOR

KEY
A   Bedroom
B   Master Bedroom
C   Bedroom
D   Bedroom
E   Bedroom
F   Bedroom

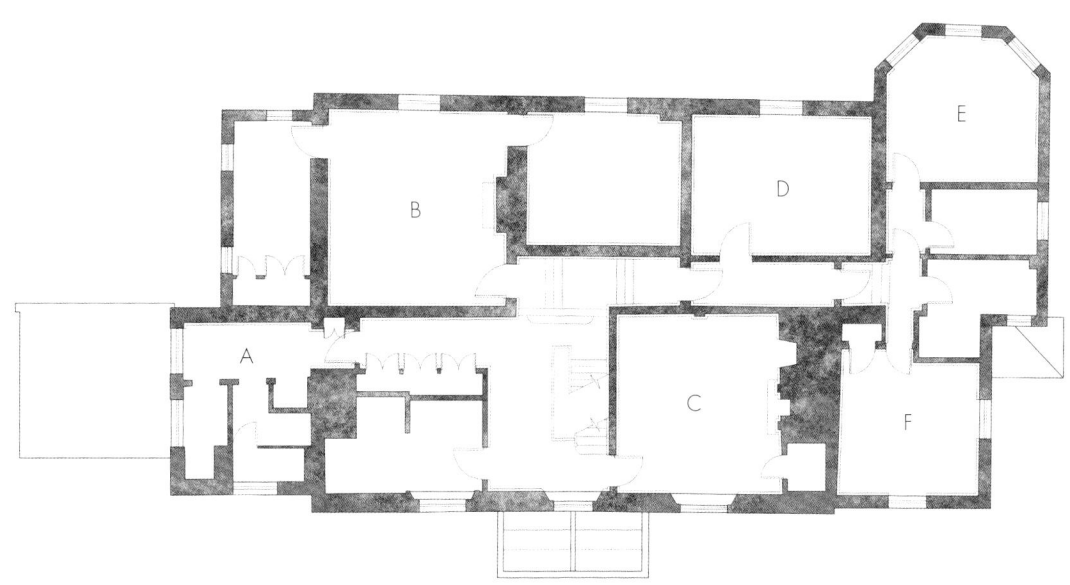

RESTORATION

BRITISH SCHOOL AT ROME
ITALY

Hugh is fortunate that in his twenties he won not one but two scholarships to the British School at Rome. This institution was founded at the beginning of the 20th century as a British equivalent to the long-established French Academy at the Villa Medici – a place where architects, artists and scholars could study the history and culture of Rome in a collegiate setting. Hugh's time there was formative. Not only did he become closely acquainted with the monuments of Rome but he could enrich his understanding through the topographical books and collections at the BSR itself – not to mention the opportunity to form friendships with art historians such as Frank Salmon, later to head the Department of History of Art at Cambridge. This provided the education in Classical architecture that he craved, after a less than wholly satisfactory experience at architecture school.

Previous spread: The British School at Rome, or BSR, which has been very important to Hugh's career.

Left: Entrance to the Sainsbury lecture theatre. It picks up the lines of the Lutyens elevation on the left hand side and integrates the late Lutyens feature of disappearing pilasters (pilasters that merge into the rustication). Wren is referenced in the segmental niche taken from St. Paul's Cathedral.

All award holders at the BSR are required to complete a project during their stay. Hugh chose to look at an aspect of Rome to which visitors are apt to close their eyes: its development after Italian unification in the late 19th century. New quarters had to be built after Rome became the capital of the country, and a city whose layout remained largely medieval had to be reordered for a more crowded age. While Hausmann's Paris became a place of new avenues and boulevards, magnificent in effect but imposed brutally on the existing urban fabric, there was neither the money nor inclination to do this in Rome, which had been chosen as the capital precisely because of its resonant history. Care was taken to insert new thoroughfares or widen others without radically disturbing the street pattern. Although he could not have known it at the time, the understanding acquired from this study prepared him for a busy practice as a masterplanner three decades later.

After leaving the BSR, Hugh retained a connection. Not only did he serve on the Faculty of the Fine Arts and the Fundraising Committee but, as a director in what was then called Robert Adam Architects, contributed to the development of the BSR's building in the grounds of the Villa Borghese. This structure had its origin in an exhibition pavilion erected by Lutyens in 1911. Based on the upper storey of the façade of St Paul's Cathedral, this proved so popular with the mayor of Rome that he offered the land at a peppercorn rent if exactly the same design could be rebuilt out of permanent materials. This work was begun in 1912, continued throughout the First World War and completed in the 1920s with various compromises due to shortage of money along the way. The result is a splendid façade, with coupled columns and pediment, grandly sited at the top of a flight of steps; behind is a somewhat more utilitarian courtyard, the west wing of which contains the library. Hugh's task was to find more space for the ever-multiplying numbers of books and to create an auditorium for lectures. The difficulties of an already exceptionally tight site were compounded by the fact that the building was protected under Rome's stringent planning laws. Furthermore, the building had already exceeded the permitted ratio of built volume to land. It must have seemed that every avenue had been blocked.

Fortunately, Hugh had studied the history of the building for a short book he wrote: *Lutyens in Italy: The Building of the British School at Rome* and therefore knew that the architect had intended to erect a colonnaded veranda along the west front: it had been jettisoned as one of the many economies that had to be made during the design process. This enabled Hugh to propose a scheme with columns and glazing which he could argue merely completed Lutyens' original vision. To his delight, the Comune di Roma accepted this argument and the library could obtain the shelf space it was predicted to need over the next decade or two. As a happy by-product of the exercise, the roof of the single-storey addition provided a magnificent terrace for the director's apartment. (With the requirement for bookshelves continuing its inexorable growth, there are now plans to make that apartment part of the library: future directors will live off-site).

The auditorium was put underground since subterranean space is easier to obtain under the planning laws than that on the surface. It still required its own entrance so that visitors from outside could attend events without disturbing the life of the School. This could be made in an otherwise blank screen wall that already existed. Again, Hugh's research had told him that Lutyens had planned an entrance on the side reached by a flight of steps. After studying both Lutyens' oeuvre and Wren's St Paul's Cathedral, Hugh proposed a scheme in which a pedimented door was set amid rustication. Above the door was a blind segmental arch derived from St Paul's. For the Doric order to either side of the door Hugh adopted an innovation that Lutyens, lover of ambiguity, had introduced to the Classical lexicon

– the disappearing pilaster. This is a pilaster whose capital is clearly visible but whose shaft has been, as it were, overwritten by the pattern of the rustication, so that it has to be intuited by the observer. Unfortunately, the thinking of the planners at that time was dictated by the pernicious Venice Charter drawn up in the 1960s to codify international practices in conservation: it states that additions to protected buildings should be in a style radically different from the original lest the unwary are tricked into thinking that the new work is genuinely old (this, it is believed by supporters, would falsify the history of the building, irrespective of the visually dystopic effect that such an approach causes). Hugh recalls the outcome of 'a long and difficult meeting' at which he showed drawings by both Lutyens and Wren: 'the upper part of the design was diluted but the lower part remained pretty much the same.' He adds, 'For me a building is a work of art and needs to be treated as such and, with the classical language, there is no reason why each generation can not add to the beauty of the whole.'

Previous spread: The main façade of the BSR, designed by Sir Edwin Lutyens. The new entrance to the Sainsbury lecture theatre can be seen on the far right. Lutyens was required to base his design on the façade of St Paul's Cathedral, by his hero Sir Christopher Wren. Hugh's work fuses Lutyens and Wren in a new synthesis which is his own style.

Right: The library veranda. This provided a much-needed extension to the reading room. Hugh's scheme is closely based on Lutyens' original intentions for the building, which helped in obtaining planning permission.

One of the new reading rooms in the library extension shown as A on the plan.

GROUND FLOOR

KEY
A   Reading Room
B   Lecture Hall

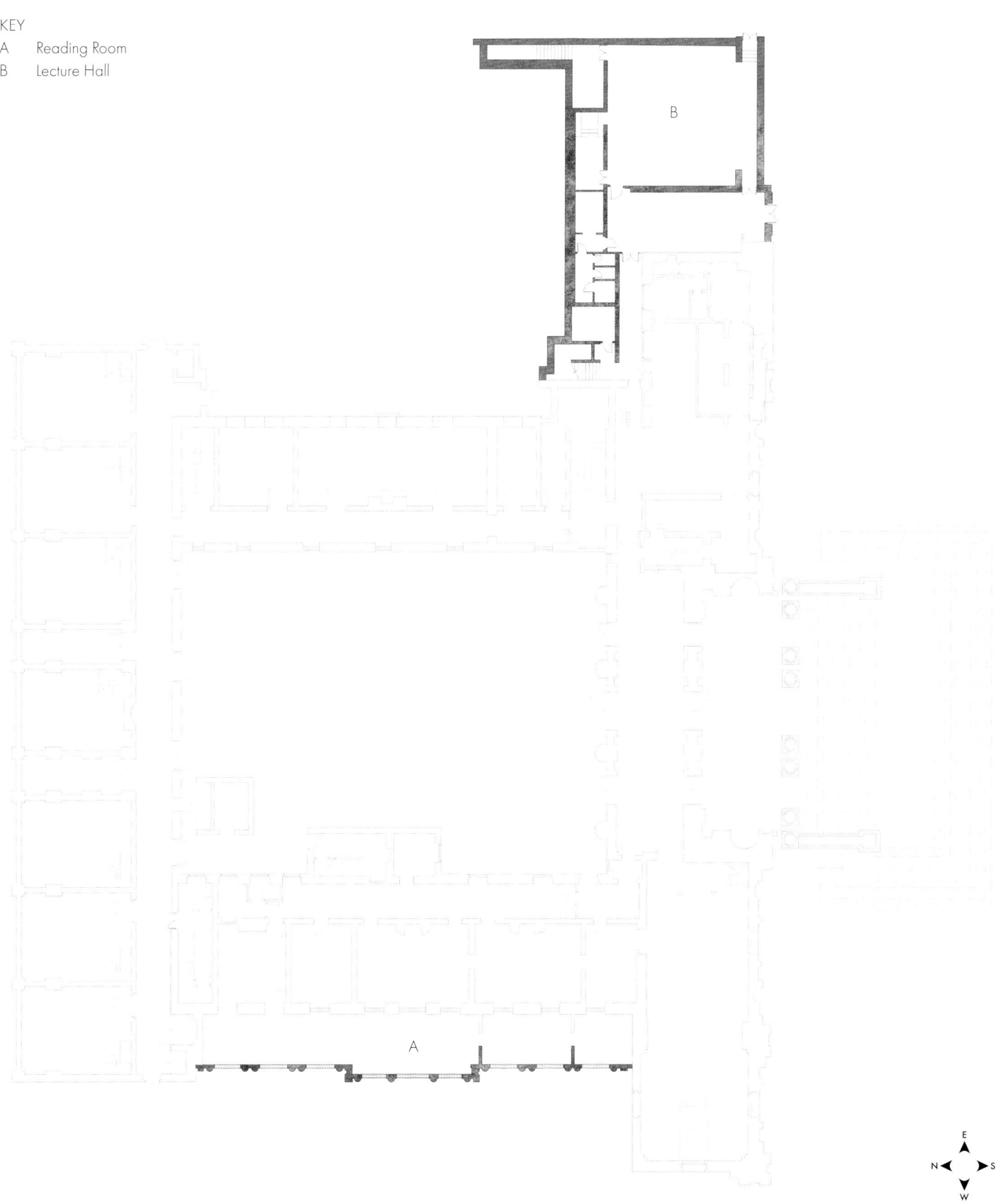

RESTORATION

A HOUSE IN HAMPSHIRE

The owners of this house remember the old one as having
'a lovely feel' to it and aimed to retain its original grandeur whilst
re-orientating it for modern life. Following this brief, Hugh
obtained planning permission for an extension which added 50%
to the existing Regency house. The new wing provided all that
was needed in terms of practical accommodation while preserving
the particular magic of an age-old family home.

As Hugh remembers: 'Our job wasn't about starting again so much as working with the ingredients we had and trying to give them the scale and character of the house the client wanted, without making it feel new. The connection between the house and the garden and the setting was very important as was having the whole thing flow in a very informal relaxed way.' The project was a collaboration between owner and architect in which the owners played a full part.

Today, the old brick wing lines one side of the entrance court; to it has been attached a new main block with Tuscan porch and pediment which might have been added during the Regency. The impressive size of the original window panes was maintained and the importance of mirroring the original glazing bars was addressed. Sash windows have been double-glazed but avoid the clumsiness that can come from the use of thick glazing bars of early-Georgian type: here they have the thin 'lamb's tongue' profile which joiners developed at the end of the 18th century (the secret is the use of rubber, rather than aluminium, gaskets to seal the units). A grand hall containing the staircase greets visitors as soon as they enter the front door. This space is divided into sections by the ceiling beams. A cornice, carefully chosen by the owners, runs around not only the walls of the room but also the beams of the ceiling, giving a sense of completeness to all three compartments. Pediments were added to the doorways, and harmonious proportions and tall ceiling heights are of the essence.

Previous spread: The new garden elevation; bracket eaves; big painted timber sash windows; lime render and Portland Stone details.

Left: A detail of one of the bays on the south elevation, showing the big sash windows with attenuated Doric pilasters. Wisteria runs riot on the free-standing colonnaded pergola between windows.

Above: Entrance elevation with the old part of the cottage on the left hand side.

A hidden lantern lights the staircase. This house is an example of what the ADAM office jokingly calls a doughnut plan, where the gloom of a deep plan is dispelled by the central top-lit staircase at the heart of the house. The quarter landing gives access to an old farmhouse wing whose ceiling heights did not correspond to those of the Regency house.

The drawing room looks south over the garden side of the house. Sash windows come down to the floor; when opened, they can be made to disappear into pockets above them leaving plenty of headroom to walk onto the terrace without ducking. Inside, the windows are flanked by shutters which fold back onto splays of wall rather than into the window embrasure, since a modern wall does not have the depth of a Georgian one. The cornice with its pattern of trailing leaves comes from the largely unchanged drawing room of the original house, from which a mould was taken.

Previous spread: View of the approach showing how the new and old part fit together.

Right: Entrance hall. The art of a cantilevered stair, as shown here, is to make the stone treads as thin as possible. The landing resolves a difference in level between the old and new parts of the building.

Left: View of the entrance hall from the front door, revealing the sense of spaciousness created by the new stairway. The etiolated metal balusters add to the refinement.

Above: View of the hall through an arched doorway.

The stairway leading to the upper floors. Elegance is achieved by keeping the cantilevered stone treads as thin as possible.

Left: From the drawing room into the garden, via one of the square bay windows. The lower sashes of some windows disappear into the wall above to allow you to walk out into the garden on a hot day.

Right: Detail of the dining room with a new Regency fireplace. There is a glimpse of the pergola through the window beyond.

Externally the window banks are separated by pilasters, with a portico of slightly bigger Doric column (the size of the Doric capitals is determined by the cornice of the pilasters). The walls are plastered with hydraulic lime render which is applied using a wooden float that leaves a slightly rough texture resembling stone and the colour was chosen accordingly, with meticulous care. Hugh's attention to materials and texture is a legacy of his interest in the Arts and Crafts movement.

As the owner freely admits, he is a man of exacting standards, whose peace of mind is put out by the slightest imperfection. Fortunately, there is nothing about the house to torment him. It is singularly calm, hung with big paintings that have been lit using the latest technology. The zen is in large part due to his wife, an interior designer. She in turn worked with Hugh on the finer points of the design, creating a harmony between architecture and decoration that not all professional designers achieve – or indeed strive after. 'The clients gave me the scope to think about the details,' says Hugh. 'Together we were able to focus on all the finer parts, from mouldings to skirting boards, that fitted with the character of the architecture and the integrity of the whole house.'

Above: Master bathroom on the first floor.

Right: The enfilade looking from the dressing room through into the master bathroom. The new shutters seen on the right show a high level of joinery.

In the new kitchen, the rectangular bay conveniently takes a dining table. There is a feeling of light and connection with the outside.

Above: The refitted boot room in the older part of the house.

Following spread: To the right of the new extension can be seen the existing brick and flint cottage.

RESTORATION

SAWMILL COTTAGE
YORKSHIRE

Hugh first met Michael Abrahams in the courtyard of the British
School at Rome one balmy evening in the early 1990s. Michael,
a successful businessman from Yorkshire, loves architecture.
He had commissioned a country house from Quinlan Terry
in the previous decade and had become chairman of
The Prince's Institute. They hit it off immediately.

In the mid 1970s Michael had built a cottage for a forester on a patch of woodland he had bought near Ripon. Designed by Malcolm Tempest, it was a pretty building with a double-hipped roof, diamond glazing bars and a rustic porch made out of logs. The stone for the walls was tooled to take render: it probably came from one of the redundant agricultural buildings that were then being knocked down. Thirty years later, when Michael's son Rupert had married his wife Philippa and a grandchild had arrived, it was decided to rehouse the forester, who was getting old, in new accommodation on the same site. Sawmill Cottage, as it was called, would take on a new life as a family home.

Michael proposed Hugh as the architect to his son and daughter-in-law. The commission was a particularly happy one for Hugh since he also had young children and understood the clients' needs. These included a large, light and airy kitchen-cum-family room with an Aga. The planners were less sympathetic. Located in an Area of Outstanding Natural Beauty, the design was scrutinised with an unusually beady eye. There was, for one thing, the question of an agricultural tie which required any new owner to be engaged with the land; this was easily overcome because, after the forester's retirement, Rupert and Philippa care for the woods themselves. The clients' desire for more living space proved more intractable. Discussions reached a nadir when one planner asked: 'Why do you need more than two bedrooms?'. The negotiation took four years, by the end of which Rupert and Philippa were well on the way to having a family of three children, not to mention several dogs and horses.

There were several design iterations. At one point, it was mooted that the new Sawmill Cottage would contain the remains of an old priory – a piece of fake history that was abandoned. The Arts and Crafts style was also tried: this was rejected because, although cosy, Arts and Crafts houses are rarely flooded with light. Instead, Hugh was inspired by the thought of a gingerbread cottage in the woods. This Hansel and Gretel effect was especially appropriate at the time of construction when fir trees came almost up to the front door. Storms have since felled a proportion of the woods, which had been neglected before Michael bought them, and the clearings turned into paddocks. The cottage orné style has the advantage that, being Picturesque, it suits an accretive plan. Sawmill Cottage grew – almost imperceptibly in terms of the front elevation – into a six bedroom house with four bathrooms. It is as though a witch had got it under her spell – a benign witch, needless to say, with a taste for Gothick windows.

The windows are what give Sawmill Cottage its character. Although the arched glazing bars represented a significant proportion of the building cost, they were too fundamental to omit and a way was found to combine them with double-glazed units. The stone slates for the new roof came, as per the requirements of the planning policies, from India. At the back of the house is a big room full of all the appurtenances of family life. It is divided by a suspended beam supported on two stumps of wall as though the space had originally been two rooms that were knocked through; this provides not only a comforting memory of numerous other family rooms across the land that have been created by this means, but breaks up what could otherwise have been a somewhat soulless structure.

Outside, stables were a priority. They have been built of breeze-block faced with waney oak (the breeze-block provides insulation). Placed at right angles to the old barn that once housed the forester and is now, since his death, a holiday let, they form a courtyard reached through an arch on the third side. The last is reached through an archway with turret and weathervane above it. The whole complex is roofed with oak shingles which, as they move with age, are a home to bats.

How was planning permission achieved for a project that the officers tried to reject? Hugh

Previous spread: An existing cottage was extended to one side and made more romantic with the addition of Gothick window bars and fretwork.

Left: The curve of the projecting entrance bay creates the opportunity for an interestingly-shaped roof.

calculated that the planning committee, made up of councillors rather than planning professionals, would take a broader view of the application. They did. Whereas architects are usually confined to a three minute slot to argue their case, Hugh, having travelled up from Winchester, found that the chairman often asked him to comment on the officer's report, allowing him to correct misunderstandings where necessary. 'It was the most civilised planning committee I've ever been to,' he remembers. The planning officers took their revenge afterwards by insisting the two walls of the 1970s cottage were retained in the rebuilding – an awkward condition in terms of the new plan, which had the further effect of classifying the work as alterations to an existing structure rather than a new build. As a result, the construction costs attracted 20% VAT.

Right: Enclosed by trees, the character of Sawmill Cottage was inspired by the idea of a gingerbread cottage in the clearing of the wood. The trees came up even more closely when the house was first altered.

Kitchen with children's chairs. Folksy colour and pattern are celebrated in the wall cabinet.

GROUND FLOOR

KEY
A Boot Room/Utility
B Kitchen
C Dining Room
D Drawing Room
E Hall
F Family Room

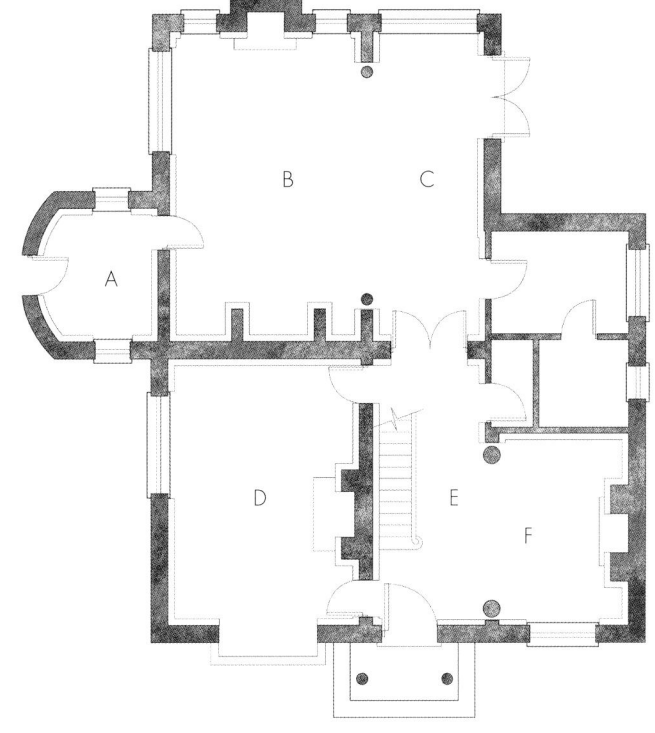

FIRST FLOOR

KEY
A Bathroom
B Bedroom
C Bedroom
D Bathroom
E Bedroom
F Bedroom

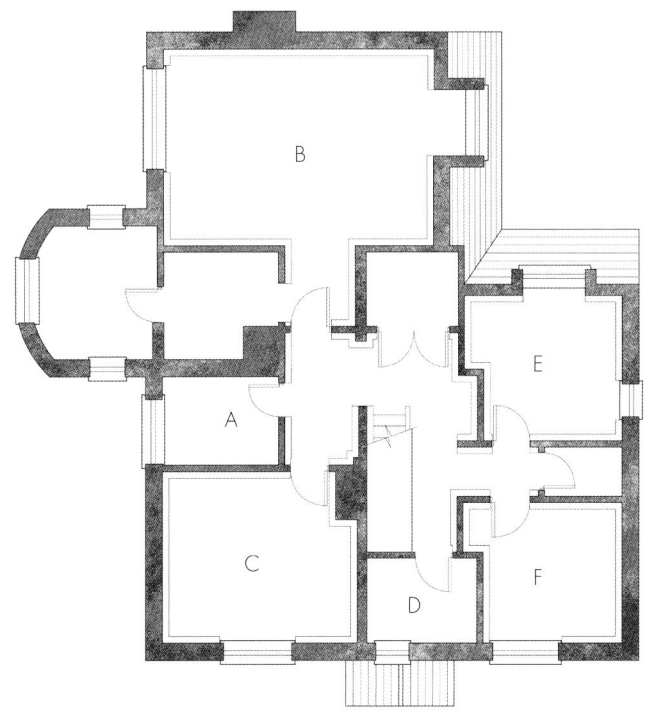

Above: Sitting room. Over the fireplace is a portrait of the owners' parents and their house.

Right: Staircase. Plain spindles, appropriate to a cottage, are elevated by the use of mahogany for the handrail.

Left: Horses rule at Sawmill Cottage. Here they watch peacefully from their specially designed stable block, with its oak boarding.

Above: The family sets out for a ride, the new flat that Hugh created (originally for a retired woodman) visible behind them.

RESTORATION

MEADOW FARM
JERSEY

'Houses are complicated things in respect of how you want to live your life.' So says Rupert Bradstock, and he should know having founded the buyer's agency Property Vision which specialises in suiting potential owners to their domestic ideal. 'I don't think people think enough about how to live in a country house. London houses are very similar to each other and can be treated as tradeable assets, but a country house is apt to be quirky and personal.'

Mr Bradstock has worked twice with Hugh, the first time in Berkshire when his and wife Anna's Old Rectory was burnt down and needed to be reconstructed. The Old Rectory is a substantial country property and he says that in living there the Bradstocks always kept an eye on the resale value. When it was time to move on to their 'forever' home, they moved not just to Jersey but to the very parish in which Anna had grown up. They found that rare thing for Jersey: an 18th-century farmhouse that had not been extended. This gave them the chance to reorganise the place as they wanted. It was in a well-wooded part of the island with the opportunity to create an outstanding garden around a pond whose banks rise up to a belt of trees on the ridge. The sea is only ten minutes away but the site is sheltered from the winds that keep Jersey's climate in a permanent state of change.

Old houses on Jersey are not generally large; they often have five bay fronts and low ceiling heights. The original Meadow Farm, built in the local rose-coloured granite, was a house of this type. However it stood on a slight rise meaning that a wing to the west could be attached, and because of the fall in the ground it would have taller rooms. The new wing, the Bradstocks decided, would be for entertaining with rooms big enough to contain inherited pictures and antiques without looking cramped, but spare in detail to avoid stuffiness. French windows along the south side of the house give access to the garden on one side and a French-style courtyard on the other: their width suggests that of barn doors, echoing those of the many converted barns on the island. After some agonising, the Bradstocks decided they did not need a dining room. Much as they had enjoyed their one at the Old Rectory, they had not actually used it to throw formal dinner parties more than a few times a year. Instead they would have a table to seat eight in the kitchen, while a refectory table in the drawing room could be pressed into service when numbers swelled. Flow was an important consideration. To avoid a bottle neck of guests as they clustered around the kitchen, a so-called scullery – practically a second kitchen – attached to a generously equipped bar has been provided; it allows the kitchen to be kept tidy as befits its use as a family room.

During the summer months Meadow Farm runs, joke the owners, 'like a small hotel with a large bar attached.' The winter months are less boisterous. With only their two grown-up children as guests, they retreat to rooms of the old farmhouse and shut the door on those intended for parties. The scale here is cosy. But the family's private space had to be made quiet. The internal structure of old Jersey houses is often wooden. This means that noise carries easily and it is always possible to know when children are playing upstairs. To avoid these evils, the ceilings and walls of Meadow Farm have been packed with acoustic padding. While the old doors have been retained, they have been made thicker, equipped with a hidden panel for sound insulation and fitted with brushes underneath as a further prevention against noise. (In doing this, the peculiarity of some doors, which are doubles of unequal width, has been retained.) Care has been taken that even the new rooms should absorb sound rather than send it bouncing back to the listener; with their uneven plasterwork, old houses are easy not just on the eye but on the ear. It adds to their sense of immemorial calm. Meadow Farm possesses the same quality.

There were other questions to consider. Most new country houses have too little 'back space,' according to Mr Bradstock; there is too little storage, meaning that the main rooms get cluttered up. Linen cupboards, properly warmed and ventilated, are required; swimmers returning from the beach need wet rooms in which they can shower. Ugly printers ought to be banned from the home office or study and hidden behind folding doors. The placing of furniture in main rooms must be thought through before, not after construction because it can be quite difficult to find space for ten or twelve chairs.

Previous page: Hugh's addition is built from materials that harmonise with the old part of the house. The stone, copying the original pink granite, is laid with tight mortar joints.

Left: The change in roof level reduces the impact of the new work. To the left can be seen the arched entrance to the new courtyard.

All these points of detail were considered during the design phase. But on an island which is fiercely protective of its traditional character, the question remained – would the scheme win over the planners? Hugh opened the campaign to do so with his usual thoroughness. This began with a detailed analysis of all the old five-bay houses on Jersey and how they had been extended over the years. Using this, he could show that the scheme he and the Bradstocks proposed was entirely in character with the island's architectural tradition. 'The evidence-based research gave us the confidence to put forward a really solid case for something special,' says Hugh. They applied for exactly what they needed, without adding the sort of unnecessary extras that are sometimes included for future use as bargaining counters. The argument proved unassailable and the plans were approved without qualification.

Right: The vernacular beauty of the 18th-century farmhouse can now be enjoyed following a comprehensive renovation.

View of the service courtyard. An area that historically housed a piggery has become an intimate, sheltered courtyard kissed by the sun.

The restored sash window comes from the old part of the house.

This small window, deeply sunk in the surrounding masonry and set at an angle, gives character to the extension.

All the work at Meadow Farm has been executed with a meticulous attention to the best materials and building methods. 'The real heroes,' says Mr Bradstock, 'were the Portuguese stone masons who carved the granite.' The quarry on Jersey is working a seam of grey granite and the pink needed at Meadow Farm could not be obtained. The planners directed the Bradstocks to Portugal where matching stone could be found. With it came four craftsmen who spent several weeks in dimpling the surface of the granite blocks to match the original walls, accompanied by rough mortar known as 'dolly pointing'. Bought in 2016, Meadow Farm was half-way through construction when the Covid pandemic reached Jersey and, for a time, building work stopped. Although it soon restarted, considerable ingenuity and some expense were needed to keep it going; the only way to bring over the German craftsmen who laid the oak floors was by private jet.

On this island of ever-changing skies, light floods in through the big windows of Meadow Farm. The rooms are comfortable and peaceful, the garden full of colour, scent and exotic plants. The formula for living, so carefully thought through by the owners, evidently works. 'When we have people here, it's hard to get rid of them,' says Mr Bradstock. Lunch guests stay into the evening. It's just what he and Mrs Bradstock like – and a tribute to the house as well as the wine cellar. 'We could not have done it without Hugh.'

Previous spread: Drawing room at Meadow Farm. The interiors are by Emily Todhunter of Todhunter Earle. Since the owners had not used the dining room much in their old house, it was decided that the drawing room could be used for dinner parties that are too big to seat in the kitchen.

Above: Back kitchen/boot room/flower room and scullery.

GROUND FLOOR

KEY
A   Store
B   Glazed Link
C   Flower Room/Scullery
D   Utility
E   Annexe Sitting Room
F   Kitchen
G   Drawing Room
H   Hall
I   Sitting Room

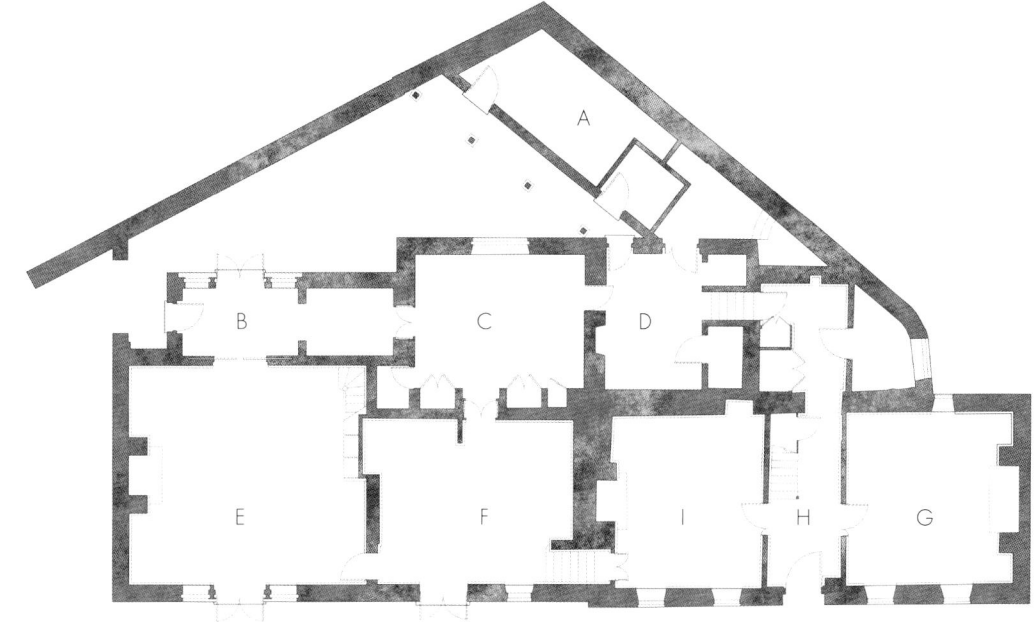

FIRST FLOOR

KEY
A   Annexe Bathroom
B   Annexe Bedroom
C   Master Bedroom
D   Bathroom
E   Dressing Room
F   Bathroom
G   Guest Room
H   Bathroom

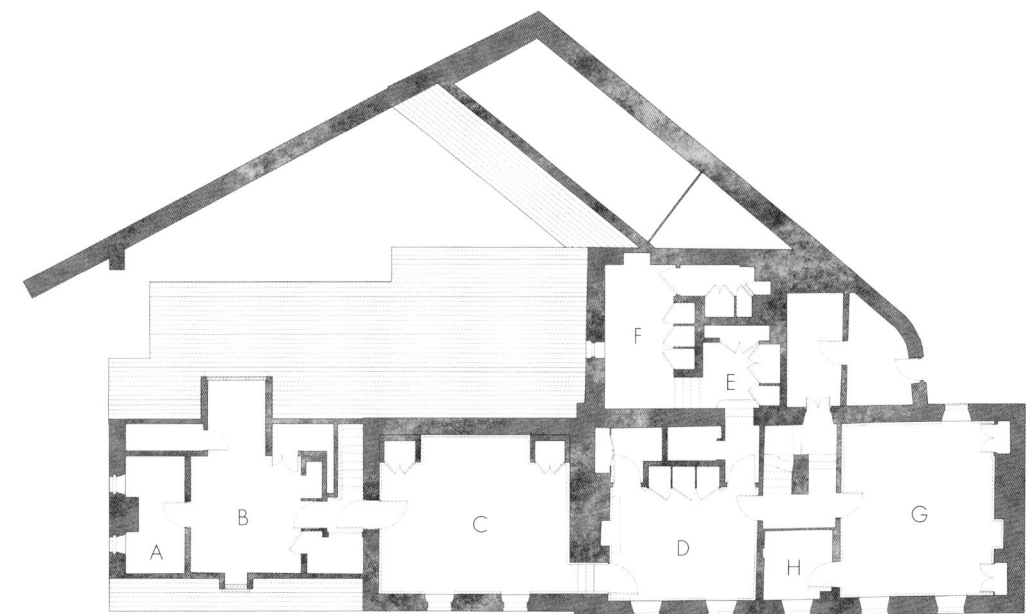

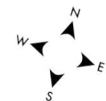

Left: View from the sitting room into the hall. Note the granite lintel. Although faced in granite, the structure of the formal part of the old house is timber-framed. The restoration renewed the pitch-pine panelling of the hall.

Above: The new kitchen shown as F on the plan.

Above: The new master bedroom gains character from its position in the roof space.

Right: Master bathroom. Both rooms enjoy views of the garden.

Following spread: Meadow Farm, Jersey in its garden setting. Hugh added the extension to the left of a five-bay 18th-century farmhouse.

PUBLIC ARCHITECTURE

PUBLIC ARCHITECTURE

THE LEVINE BUILDING
TRINITY COLLEGE, OXFORD

Hugh's commission to design a major new block for Trinity College, Oxford, came through friends made while fundraising for the British School at Rome who were also working at Oxford. From them he learned that the College wanted to expand on its historic site, and this led to a visit, followed by dinner at high table; having returned to Winchester, he produced a series of drawings that explored the possibilities. This was the beginning of a design phase that lasted nearly a decade.

Page 198/199: View of the garden through the Wilderness, Trinity College, Oxford.

Previous spread: Front elevation of the Levine Building. The different treatment of the window surrounds is a simple means of giving hierarchy to the building, without undue ornament.

The new building abuts the War Memorial Library, seen here on the right. The cornice line is maintained and the scale of the windows echoed in the new.

Initially, it seemed that a new range might be erected close to the college boundary. The possible new site lay adjacent to a 1920s library (erected as a memorial to alumni who had fallen during the First World War) and an area of wild garden known as the Wilderness: a patch of open space within the Tudor precincts of the College which contained a memory of a 17th-century landscape (replacement trees mark the line of a lime avenue). Hugh's proposal served as a catalyst. Trinity held a competition between a spectrum of architects, including Hugh, whose understanding of the site, developed through his previous work, helped him win it. At that stage, his scheme hugged the boundary of the college so as not to impinge on whatever open space remained to the college on its restricted site. For reasons of economy, it kept the demolition of existing architecture to a minimum.

However, this plan did not endear itself to such college neighbours as the Bodleian Library and Wadham College. Ultimately a solution was provided by the decision to demolish an unloved 1960s pagoda-like structure known as Staircase 4 which stood next to the library. This gave Hugh the opportunity to create what is practically a new quad. His work has been named as the Levine Building in honour of the parents of Peter Levine, a former student of Trinity who chaired the construction engineering companies Severfield-Rowen Plc and Keltbray Plc.

Responding to the College's strong desire for contemporary architecture, Hugh's design is in a Modern Classical style inspired by Grey Wornum's RIBA building at 66 Portland Place. Rather than fighting its surroundings by adopting an aggressively different palette of materials, it is, to quote President of Trinity, Dame Hilary Boulding, 'polite'; it respects the historic character of the College and, like the other elements of this five hundred-year-old institution, has been built to last. Honey-coloured ashlar limestone walls and Classical proportions are combined with deep windows in bronzed frames made by Crittall.

Oak is much used in the interior in conjunction with unusually tall ceiling heights. There is little of the ornament that a New Classicist might have applied in the 1980s or 1990s. This development of the Classical language could be of relevance to numerous other projects where elegance without an undue overload of extraneous detail is sought.

For the College, the result provides both openness and flexibility. While Trinity has always shown a glimpse of itself through the wrought-iron gates of 1737 on Broad Street, the architecture, like that of other Oxford colleges, forms a series of quads whose enclosed nature did not encourage interaction with the public. The facilities available in the new range will make the College more outward-facing. They include a new auditorium to which the public can be welcomed for concerts or plays. For Fellows of the College this can double as a lecture theatre where they can share their erudition with audiences of all kinds. To help meet these different needs, the walls of the auditorium are lined with fin-like acoustic baffles that can be opened or closed depending on the purpose to which the room is being put. Exceptional care was taken to provide every seat with a good view of the stage. This was partly achieved through a programme of empirical research conducted around the theatres of other Oxford colleges. During these visits, Dame Hilary (being petite) would sit behind Hugh who is six foot six: if she could still see the stage the configuration was judged to have worked.

Forty-six study bedrooms have been provided for undergraduate students, freeing up rooms to house postgraduate students on site. The accommodation allows for participation in college life, which is an essential component of the Oxford experience. These bedrooms are spacious and each floor has a well-equipped kitchen since not all students want to eat in hall and, besides, cooking will for some be a valuable means of interaction. Beneath the beds are large, lockable storage spaces so that students do not

The library is now entered through the new block. The inscription on the lintel of the door remembers its role as a war memorial.

The north end of the Levine Building provides a sense of enclosure, effectively creating a new quad.

need to transport all their possessions to and fro at the start and end of each term – a major consideration in the case of families who do not have a car or cannot take time off work to drive to Oxford on the requisite days. Opening windows bring sunlight and fresh air into the accommodation, which increase the occupants' sense of well-being. This is a low-energy building. The building's structural frame takes the form of concrete walls, cast in-situ, to which is attached a free-standing outer skin made of stone. Since the external envelope takes most of the weight of the building, it will be possible for the plan to be reconfigured over time if needs change. The gap between the concrete and the stone prevents water penetration, while the high thermal mass keeps the building cool in summer as well as warm in winter: nowhere is there a need for air-conditioning except in the auditorium (where open windows would allow disturbance from noise) and an underground kitchen that serves events.

Crucially the Levine Building also provides workspaces appropriate to the age of the laptop. 21st-century students are not only used to more communal styles of working than previous generations but, even when working alone, like to do so in the company of others. So an attractive and well-stocked café is essential if Trinity students are not to drift off to coffee shops elsewhere in town. At the junction with the War Memorial Library is a mezzanine that serves as an antechamber with desks: more intimate than the lofty, vaulted space of the library proper, it has proved popular with students. If the proximity of the Levine Building initially made the library look shabby, never fear: every book has been subsequently removed as part of a major renovation.

Right: Aerial view across the Trinity College lawn, showing the relationship of the Levine Building – seen here through trees – to the historic city. The Bodleian Library, the Sheldonian Theatre and the Radcliffe Camera can all be seen.

Part of the muscular balustrade on the northern wing. It provides a boundary to a new roof terrace.

Above: Arch and walkway connecting the Wilderness with the service yard. Entrances to the garden room and teaching rooms give off it.

Right: Here the façade is faced in rubblestone to accord with a service building that originally housed the President's chauffeur, seen with the scroll gable on the left hand side of this view. A previously scruffy space has been given order by being made into a small court.

Left: The stage uses profiled oak to create a perfect acoustic, whatever the performance.

Above: Vertical slats can be opened and closed to change the acoustics: open gives a drier acoustic for spoken word; closed they make a more reverberant room for music.

The raked seating in the auditorium, carefully designed to allow good sight lines and enough legroom.

Previous spread: A view of the auditorium from the stage. The coffering in the ceiling conceals air conditioning and ventilation.

Above: The Garden Room, with tall windows looking onto greenery, is used for many purposes including meetings, seminars and small lectures.

The café provides an informal space where students can work on their laptops (better for them to be on site, reinforcing the college environment, than in commercial coffee shops outside); it is also somewhere used by all members of the college, allowing all year groups as well as Fellows to interact.

PUBLIC ARCHITECTURE

MILLENNIUM GATE
ATLANTA, USA

Everything conspires against the building of a triumphal arch in the 21st century. Apart from the people who say it cannot be done, there is a Modernist architectural establishment that regards historical reference as a crime. And yet occasionally a client of vision will emerge who is prepared to do battle with these daunting odds. One such is Rodney Mims Cook, Jr. of Atlanta.

Previous spread: The Millennium Gate is in the middle of a revitalised quarter of Atlanta, masterplanned by DPZ.

Left: This triumphal arch sits at the end of a garden in the middle of the Atlantic Station scheme. It celebrates 2,000 years of peaceful endeavour. Over the main cornice are palm fronds symbolising peace.

Founder of the National Monuments Foundation, Mr Cook approached Hugh in the early 2000s about the design of an arch to stand on the site of Atlantic Station in Atlanta, Georgia. One had already been designed as a permanent commemoration of the Millennium for Washington D.C., where it was to have stood on Commodore Barney Circle. Part of Pierre Charles L'Enfant's original plan for the city, although not constructed until 1903, the Circle connects the John Philip Souza Bridge with Pennsylvania Avenue, and an arch there would have formed an important gateway to the nation's capital. Mr Cook was a member of the board of The Prince of Wales's charitable foundation in the USA: The Prince of Wales's Foundation for Architecture. This group supported The Prince of Wales's Institute of Architecture in the UK (as it was then known). He already had experience of monument building and the complex planning issues that often surround it, having taken the lead in erecting The Prince of Wales's World Athletes Monument in Atlanta to commemorate the Centennial Olympic Games of 1996. He had seen how the building of a monument can give identity to an uncertain neighbourhood and generate improvement. Despite fierce opposition from the Modernist faction, the Washington arch received the necessary permits and construction was ready to begin when the world was overturned by the 9/11 attack on the Pentagon. There followed a terrorist campaign involving anthrax: nothing would be built until Washington's security had been reassessed.

Not wanting to lose the fruits of so much work entirely, Mr Cook proposed relocating the scheme on a slightly smaller scale to his home city of Atlanta. His Board of Directors agreed. A site was provided by Jim Jacoby and Mark Toro of North American Properties who were developing the former steel mill of Atlantic Station into a restaurant and shopping destination, with help from the New Urbanist firm of Duany Plater-Zyberk & Co. (DPZ). Hugh, already known to Mr Cook from his work for The Former Prince of Wales, was commissioned to oversee the project. The result is the Millennium Gate: a triumphal arch that rises seventy feet, containing period room settings as part of a Georgian history museum inside. Constructed of Indiana limestone, it was America's first urban monument of this scale since the building of the Jefferson Memorial in 1939 (indeed, so little familiar were the Atlanta authorities with the idea of a triumphal arch that they struggled to understand why, in planning terms, the building had a hole in it). The restrictions of the oval site precluded setting the arch axially on 17th Street, the divided highway that leads up to it: the size of the road would in any case have required an even bigger structure to dominate it. Instead, in the picturesque tradition, it is placed at an angle, leading the eye around the street's change of direction. The off-centre relationship to the boulevard recalls the setting of many ancient monuments in Rome.

Before the arch was constructed two eight-foot-high statues by the Scottish sculptor Alexander Stoddart had already arrived: the figures of Peace and Justice represent the civilising values that preside over the urban regeneration of Atlantic Station. Cast in Hampshire, they were sent to Atlanta's port, Savannah, by ship; from there the bronzes began a Monumental Journey, drawn on a caisson by Percheron horses, which took them to ten cities. The sculptor himself, wearing a kilt, led them triumphantly to the site accompanied by the sound of bagpipes. Peace shows Eirene, Greek goddess of Peace, with her hand resting on the shoulder of the young Plutos who represents wealth – for peace must nurture wealth. Justice is personified by the goddess Dike wearing Egyptian clothes to portray the antiquity and universality of the concept.

At a late stage in the design process, a temple to house Mr Cook's office and provide a highly desirable space for entertaining was introduced to the scheme, not wholly to Hugh's delight; but triumphal arches have taken many different forms over the centuries – Admiralty Arch on London's Mall leading to Buckingham Palace incorporates offices for naval administration and is now being converted to a hotel – and it could be argued (as Mr Cook does) that the Millennium Gate in this respect represents another stage in the evolution of this long-lived architectural idea.

In 2006 the gate won a Palladio Award in the Public Spaces category.

Right: In Alexander Stoddart's sculpture on the right, Justice is personified by the Greek goddess Dike, wearing Egyptian clothes to portray the antiquity and universality of the concept. She was cast in Basingstoke, in Hampshire, and transported to Atlanta by ship and horse-drawn carriage.

At the back, the arch rises above a sunken garden, which gives access to the museum inside.

The interior galleries of the museum were designed by Rodney Mims Cook, Jr. and the period rooms by Lady Henrietta Spencer-Churchill.

PUBLIC ARCHITECTURE

STOCKS GOLF CLUBHOUSE
HERTFORDSHIRE

A theme of Hugh's work is the maximising of assets. At Stocks House, formerly owned by Victor Lownes of the Playboy Club, the new owner, Peter Harris, found a golf clubhouse situated inconveniently beside the house. Golf, however, remained an important activity both to Peter and his family and to the members of Stocks Golf Club. Hugh was approached to provide a new club house in a more convenient location. This was easier said than done, since the estate occupies an idyllic Hertfordshire location – in the Green Belt adjacent to both land owned by the National Trust and an exceptionally pretty village – and the most sensible site lay in the middle of the golf course, a more or less green field site. Planning lasted five years, ending in an appeal. Fortunately, the planning inspector was won over.

This must have been in large measure due to the sympathetic nature of Hugh's design, a homage to the golf clubhouse that Sir Edwin Lutyens designed for his brother-in-law Lord Lytton at Knebworth.

Like the Knebworth clubhouse, Stocks is created from a vernacular palette of clapperboard and clay tile. As Hugh comments: 'The building is designed in an H plan with a hipped roof to minimise its impact on the sensitive countryside location, and is also highly sustainable using local materials for the oak frame.' Beneath the gable, at either end of the main front, is a large Venetian window, handsome in itself but also practical in terms of light being let through into the principal rooms. Between them, the roof comes down low over a veranda – a sheltered spot from which to survey the state of play on the course. Three small dormers put their heads almost cheekily out of the slope of the roof. Above them the whole composition is completed by a clock tower. The jauntiness that is appropriate to a sporting pavilion has been combined with a self-evident love of the Classical tradition and local materials. Which is what Hugh's oeuvre is all about.

Previous spread: Stocks Golf clubhouse was inspired by the Lutyens clubhouse at nearby Knebworth.

Right: The front elevation showing clock tower and Diocletian windows. The deep roofs and dormers evoke Lutyens.

Left: The clubhouse takes the form of an embellished H-shaped barn with classical features.

Right: A large Diocletian window overlooking the final tee.

PUBLIC ARCHITECTURE 229

GROUND FLOOR

KEY
A   Dining Room
B   Drinks/Cellar
C   Kitchen
D   Lounge/Bar/Function Room
E   Administration Office
F   Hall
G   Female WC's
H   Male WC's
I   Changing Facilities
J   Entrance Lobby
K   Changing Facilities

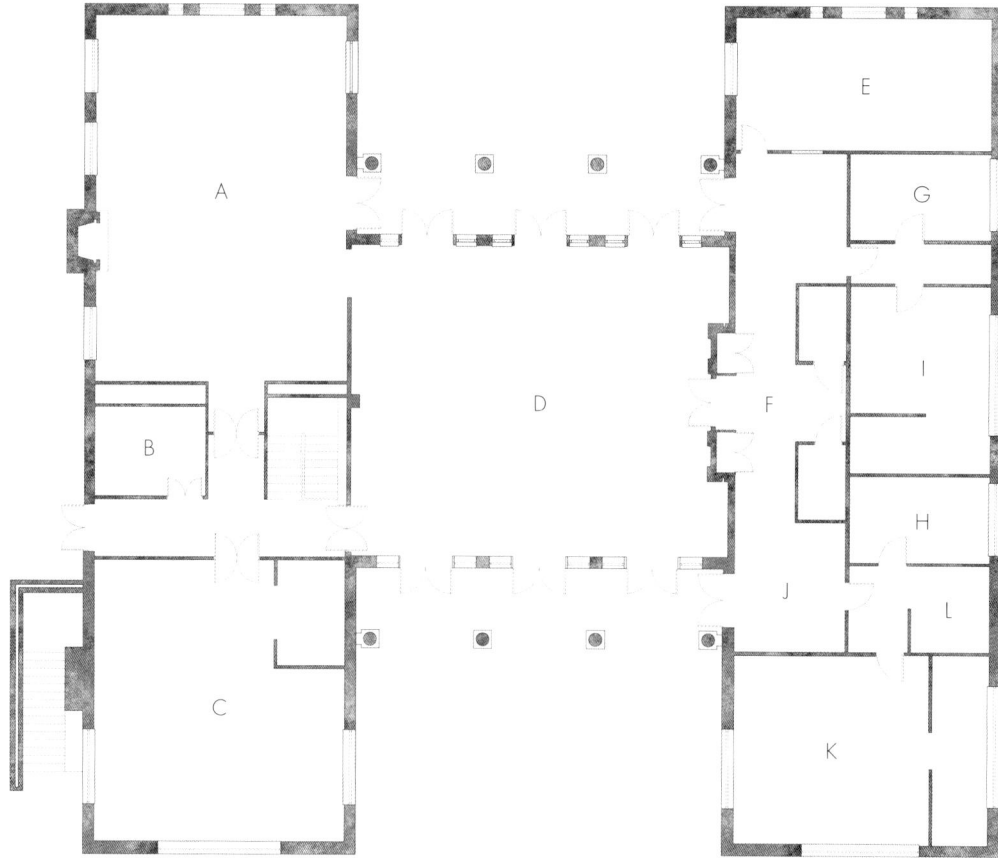

Detail of the colonnaded side entrance and porch.

Tall chimneys provide a vertical accent.

Left: The traditional barn-like frame of the bar was constructed from green oak.

Above: The clubhouse in its idyllic location, with the wooded hills of Hertfordshire beyond. The building won its appeal to sit on the land, because its character was in keeping with the landscape in this Area of Outstanding Natural Beauty.

PUBLIC ARCHITECTURE

196A PICCADILLY
LONDON

196a Piccadilly began life as a branch of the Midland Bank, for which Sir Edwin Lutyens worked extensively after the First World War. Built of red brick with flamboyant stone dressings on a square plan, it may seem to be a homage to Sir Christopher Wren, whose church of St James's, Piccadilly, stands next door. In fact this exuberant and intensely architectural building owes as much to the Italian architect Michele Sanmichele, whose Porta San Zeno at Verona bears striking similarities, as it does to Hugh's English hero. This architectural jewel was treasured by successive directors of the Midland Bank as befitted its grade 2* listing; but when the Midland became part of HSBC in the 1990s, it fell victim to corporate mistreatment.

Not only was an ATM machine crudely inserted onto the Piccadilly façade but the walnut panelling of the banking hall was butchered and the so-called American Room on the first floor – an elegant panelled space finished in limed oak with bold bolection mouldings – was dismantled. While some parts of panelling were squirrelled away in dusty corners of the building, others disappeared. Admirers of Lutyens mourned.

Happily, when the Bank's lease came to an end and the building reverted to Westminster City Council, Hugh was asked to restore it. 'Having recently finished my work at the BSR,' he remembers, 'the opportunity to restore another important building by one of my great architect heroes was almost too good to be true!' With his colleague Ed Taylor, a former student of his at The Prince of Wales's Institute of Architecture, he set about a forensic survey of the main architectural spaces within the building focused upon the banking hall and the American Room. Westminster's plan was to advertise the building for the same planning use class as the bank and then, if no taker came forward, change the use to a restaurant. It was thought that the banking hall would make a magnificent dining hall and the American Room an elegant private dining room.

Previous spread: Entrance to the jewel box that is Lutyens' 196a Piccadilly, previously a bank. Hugh oversaw the removal of the cash machine and removed and repaired the brickwork.

Right: The orangey brick of 196a Piccadilly, now a bookshop, contrasts with the more mulberry-coloured walls of St James's, Piccadilly. Although the latter was designed by Lutyens' hero Wren, his own design was inspired by Sanmichele. Hugh's restoration has returned its sparkle.

Another associate from The Prince of Wales's architectural circle was introduced to the project in the shape of Dick Reid, the master carver from York. Together Hugh and Reid reassembled what they could from the surviving fragments of panelling, and then Reid and his team skilfully patched in the missing material. By the time they had finished, most people would not have known that any intervention had taken place. 'For some architects, such an approach is anathema as they feel the need to leave their stamp on everything they do. But for me,' says Hugh, 'a building is a work of art and the ego of the architect should be suppressed as it is the beauty of the whole that should matter more.'

After restoration, 196a Piccadilly did not become a restaurant but an art gallery for the contemporary dealers Hauser and Wirth. Alas, they put up plain white walls within the main architectural spaces and so the building remained for a decade. When Hauser and Wirth left, the bookshop Maison Assouline took the lease. Once more Lutyens' beautiful rooms, equally beautifully restored, could be seen by the public. The result is an architectural treat.

Left: Above the display cases can be seen the original restored galleried landing and clock.

Above: The revival of the interiors has allowed them to be used for a new purpose.

Following spread: What was the main banking hall had become badly degraded. Hugh located the old walnut panelling in a store room, put it back together and replaced the substantial amounts that were missing or unusable. As ever with his work, the object was to give the impression that no intervention had taken place.

MASTERPLANNING & URBAN DESIGN

MASTERPLANNING & URBAN DESIGN

NANSLEDAN AND TREGUNNEL HILL
CORNWALL

Several elements in Hugh's career prepared him for Nansledan, the Duchy of Cornwall's model town (actually an urban extension) outside Newquay in Cornwall. They include his study of the transformation of Rome after the Unification of Italy made while he was at the British School at Rome; the understanding that Rome gave him of how traditions evolve; his exposure to the ethos of the Arts and Crafts movement through the Art Workers' Guild; and his work as a tutor for The Prince's Foundation which caught the eye of The Former Prince of Wales. Nansledan was prefigured by the smaller development of Tregunnel Hill where the ideas were tried out in collaboration with Ben Pentreath and the Cornish architect Peter Hume. The first sod at Tregunnel Hill was turned in 2012; Nansledan is expected to take another thirty years to complete.

Page 242/243: An aerial view of the Duchy of Cornwall's Tregunnel Hill, in Cornwall, with Newquay in the background.

Previous spread: Looking down a lane at Tregunnel Hill. Down the centre of the road runs a granite rill. Note the slate-hanging on the right.

Left: Pebbledash and Art Deco detailing with a characteristically bold use of colour. Every detail of the project was reviewed by The Former Prince of Wales who took a keen interest.

Projects of this kind require a long-term commitment from the landowner, which is why – unlike so much of the housing provided by volume house builders in the UK – the result will be a community, with thoughtfully designed streets, attractive planting, locally sourced materials, garden squares and allotments that make it a desirable place to live.

Nansledan follows the Duchy's famous model development of Poundbury outside Dorchester, now thirty years old. Poundbury demonstrated the virtues of walkable, mixed-use neighbourhoods, in which the car is subservient to pedestrian, push-chair and bike. These were radical ideas in the 1980s, and they have had a profound, if sometimes unacknowledged influence on the planning system. In the public mind, though, Poundbury is associated more with architectural style – traditional streets and squares, on which Classical buildings are prominent – than the principles that underlie it. A different approach has been taken at Nansledan. Architecturally the mood is quieter. The terraces are created from a limited palette of materials and colours, controlled by the provisions of the masterplan: sparkle is added by judicious expenditure on the more prominent sites. There is greater emphasis on sustainability in all its forms, from local food hubs to supporting the local economy through a commitment to Cornish granite and slate. Although traditional in appearance, the approach is innovative. Nansledan is proving popular, not least with young buyers.

Modernists might prefer a more obviously contemporary result – but that doesn't affect the planning principles which, curiously, aren't very different from those of the apostle of high tech, the late Richard Rogers (Lord Rogers of Riverside). Besides, while the Duchy of Cornwall's new homes could have been made to look shiny and cool, using prefabricated panels made in distant factories, there are benefits to traditional building beyond disputed aesthetics. The use of local bricklayers, carpenters, roofers, plumbers and electricians creates local employment. This is particularly important in an area of deprivation such as Cornwall.

In 2017, the Grenfell Tower fire threw a spotlight onto affordable accommodation which fails to meet basic safety standards, as well as the perils of materials such as cladding whose properties cannot be intuitively understood. The obvious difference between the haves and have-nots in Kensington and Chelsea has stirred fury. Policy-makers wanting to heal these wounds should visit Nansledan, 30% of which is affordable. You would not know it though. Low cost, rented homes are scattered among the more expensive, owner-occupied ones, with no visible difference between them.

Tim Gray, who was the Duchy of Cornwall's estate surveyor for nearly two decades, describes the vision. 'How society chooses to house people is every bit as important as how it chooses to feed people. If you can get those two things right you will be both happier and healthier, and better able to engage socially so as to be a contributor as opposed to a burden on the state and the planet.' The inhabitants of Nansledan can meet their daily needs on foot; their homes are connected 'socially and positively with the adjacent settlements'; and the qualities that people like in the architecture will be secured for the future through a Design and Community Code. At a time when the nation is debating how to build large numbers of new homes, Nansledan shows, in Gray's words, that 'there really is an alternative' to the standard offering of the volume house builders.

As masterplanner, Hugh sets the theme for Nansledan, working alongside the landowner. He has explained what this means in an article for *ANTA: Archives of New Traditional Architecture*, the house magazine of the University of Notre Dame's School of Architecture.

Masterplans, in essence, are movement networks, and the final form of each urban block is only determined when that phase of development comes forward. In this way, each phase of development is well attuned to the current property market, so helping to husband long term value. The nature of these movement networks should reflect established regional character to help ensure that the development feels like it belongs to its setting in terms of the widths and attributes of each type of street; the scale of squares; the relationship to topography; the prevailing weather, and so on.

As part of the vision principles, long term sustainable strategies should be developed for energy, transport, green infrastructure, employment, play, food and water. These need to be kept under review over the life of the development to embrace change and to ensure that standards continue to rise. The ambition should be to strengthen and diversify the local economy by responding to local needs and to put as much money from the development as possible back into the local community so that those most affected by it enjoy the resulting economic warmth. Sustainable development is not just about the delivery of low carbon houses, it is about the creation of places which enable low carbon patterns of living.

Right: Run of cottages in front of an established farm hedge. The old farm track has been laid with granite chips and edged with a lavender hedge to become a pedestrian and cycle route.

Following spread: The streets of Nansledan from above, showing brightly painted homes and narrow pedestrian and cycle-friendly curved roads.

Left: This house has been finished in Callywith Stone from Bodmin. Special treatment is reserved for buildings in eye-catching positions. They lift the character of a development, most of which is low-key. The keystone was designed by Charles Gurrey. In the foreground can be seen a Cornish hedge: vegetation emerges from a stone-sided bank.

Above: One of the secondary streets. The hooped railings are copied from the railings at the Duchy estate in Kennington in South London.

The Design Code the architecture reflects the particular character of each street in terms of form, massing, set back, architectural detail and public realm materials, and that the green infrastructure is properly woven through the development. This sets the parameters within which the West Country house builders can operate: Morrish Homes, CG Fry & Son and Wain Homes, who buy parcels of land from the Duchy and build out the development. A number of different house types have been set down, giving the house builders the freedom to meet market demand; they must, however, always conform to the pattern of public realm laid down in the contract. This, says Hugh, is not so different from the way Georgian cities such as Bath were developed: builders conformed to predetermined street elevations but were free to do what they liked at the back.

A particularly prominent building – perhaps on a junction or at the end of a view – may be given extra emphasis, by means of a Classical porch or slate-hung façade; and some fun has been had with monuments, such as an obelisk which is justified as a traffic calming measure. The feel generally, is understated, and more akin to a genuine vernacular than other housing developments. In addition, the hilly topography of Nansledan and Tregunnel Hill encourages a natural variety.

Above, left: Zinc seahorse ornament, made in France, on an Art Deco-style building.

Above: Detail of a wall-hung street lamp. In narrow roads wall-hung lighting creates a more intimate feel.

Right: One of the mixed use buildings with a bakery on the ground floor and flats overhead. The bicoloured window frames are a cheap means of lifting the visual interest of the building.

Local residents gather at a popular cafe in Nansledan, designed by Hugh, where independent businesses are thriving. The town has been planned so that locals can meet their daily needs on foot within a short distance of their homes.

There is plenty of outdoor space for dog walking and flying kites. Thoughtfully designed streets, attractive planting, locally sourced materials, garden squares and allotments make Nansleden a desirable place to live.

Previous spread: Art Deco building designed by Hugh at the entrance to Nansledan. The roundabout in the foreground supports a granite obelisk.

Above: This Art Deco building designed by George Saumarez Smith may be simple but strong colours bring it to life.

Inscription on the obelisk at Nansledan, designed by Charles Gurrey. The dramatic font is derived from 1930s Italy.

Aerial view of the local centre at Kosti Veur in Nansledan. While many high streets are struggling, commercial properties at Nansledan's are in high demand.

Site plan for Nansledan. Areas yet to be developed are shown as an outline.

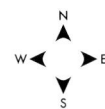

MASTERPLANNING & URBAN DESIGN

Before work began, a careful study was made of seaside vernacular which revealed that the building types were often simple but enlivened with coloured walls and cheerfully painted doors and window frames. Art Deco, calculated to raise the spirits at a minimum of cost, its repertoire of relatively simple forms being executed in cement, had an affinity with holiday places in the age of mass tourism. It has become one of the themes of Nansledan. There was some concern that details such as the Art Deco seahorse (made, exceptionally, in a workshop in Paris that specialises in decorative zinc) would horrify The Former Prince of Wales, who takes a keen interest in every building. Instead he was charmed. As for the colours in which it was proposed to paint the streets, he simply said, 'Make them bolder.'

Nansledan is a Cornish word meaning broad valley. To encourage a sense of local identity, all the street names – Gwarak Agravayn, Bownder Marhaus and Stret Morgan Le Fay – are Cornish too. They remember local field names or evoke tales of Arthurian romance (Tintagel, where King Arthur was supposedly conceived, is 30 miles away). These names are carved into tablets of Delabole slate. The curbs of the street are edged with Cornish granite, from a nearby quarry that has been given a new lease of life. The quarry provides local jobs. The use of West Country builders creates local employment and helps to establish local supply chains.

It may be that we don't hear so much about localism now as in the heyday of the Localism Act, 2011, but it is part of Nansledan, the whole idea of which is to meet local need. Newquay has a quite different demographic from Dorchester, the county town to which Poundbury is attached. If it were not for its popularity with surfers, there would be little industry. There is a strong local need for housing, particularly among young people. Nansledan answers it. Superfast broadband is provided throughout, making it possible for young parents to work more from home, and entrepreneurs to spend more time in the community while travelling to London or elsewhere perhaps once or twice a week. Like California, Cornwall is lifestyle-focused, with a greater openness to the green agenda than some metropolitan areas. This appeals to young families who respond to Nansledan's edible gardens (herbs and fruit bushes are planted next to houses); espaliered pear trees; bee bricks (bricks with holes that are laid into the eaves of houses to welcome threatened bee populations); and RSPB approved swift boxes to attract nesting swifts.

As well as local style, local materials and local employment – local food. This is symbolised by community orchards and a number of sites, given by the Duchy, that have been energetically (and back-breakingly) turned into allotments. Orchard and allotments are only the visible sign of the local food web that is being encouraged by a 54-page food strategy document. And they do more than reduce food miles: placed on the edge of the development, orchards and allotments are somewhere that people from Nansledan meet long-time Newquay residents. 'Place-making' is a buzzword among thoughtful planners. We have not generally been very good at it in Britain in recent times, but Nansledan shows what can be done.

On the 500 or so acres that comprise Nansledan and Tregunnel Hill, the Duchy is creating something over 4,000 homes. House buyers must sign a Design and Community Code covenant requiring them to maintain their home and an element of the public realm in accordance with the Duchy's vision. This may seem restrictive, but the knowledge that the development is being aesthetically policed and that everyone is subject to the same restraints gives them confidence that the things they like about Nansledan will not change. This is reflected in the premium they are willing to pay over equivalent new homes elsewhere. Resale values are higher too. For Nansledan has so much more to offer than a standard housing estate whose developer moves on as soon as he has built and sold the

Previous spread: Curving street in Tregunnel Hill with a prominent building highlighted with hung slate.

Right: Homes in Tregunnel Hill and Nansledan are hotly competed for. This side street shows the use of Cornish slate, granite and coastal plants.

Left: Children walk down a pavement edged with granite. In an area of housing need, homes here have proved popular with young families.

Above: A carefully detailed door case, with leadwork over the hood, tucked into the render.

Timber detailing raises the character of the street. A row of cottages with fisherman's porches made of weatherboarding.

properties. The Duchy of Cornwall takes the long view. Committed to maintaining quality, the development progresses at the most sustainable rate. At present only about 100 houses come onto the market in any year. A necessary rate due to a limited supply of the materials, the building skills required and the rate of absorption with the local property market. As a result, it will take decades for the whole site to be built out – a time scale that is inconceivable to volume house-builders such as Persimmon. This, however, is central to the Duchy model. While it invests heavily in the early years, it knows – because Poundbury has confirmed this – that the value of its land will go up, and it will more than recoup the initial expenditure through later land sales and income from commercial lettings.

Right: Coastal planting provides cheer and a sense of local identity to the fronts of houses in Tregunnel Hill.

This aerial view of Tregunnel Hill shows community gardens adjoining a mixed use Art Deco building.

Site plan for Tregunnel Hill. Areas yet to be developed are shown as an outline.

MASTERPLANNING & URBAN DESIGN

PARK VIEW
OXFORDSHIRE

Oxfordshire is one of Britain's most expensive counties for house-buyers. At Woodstock, the Blenheim estate has responded to the pressure by instigating its own urban extension called Park View. This will comprise three hundred new homes initially, and possibly more in due course. Cheaper housing is badly needed around the boom city of Oxford, if only to encourage young people to live there and service the local economy. Masterplanned by Hugh, Park View is meant to bring fresh blood to a town whose many charms have brought an affluent but older population.

Page 275: One of the larger new houses in Park View, outside Woodstock, in Oxfordshire, built of Cotswold Stone and an artificial stone slate called Cardinal.

Previous spread: CGI image of what will be the town square at the centre of the scheme, with commercial space on the ground floor of the buildings, and apartments above. With an obelisk in the middle, it will become the centre of the urban extension in due course.

Left: Another house in Park View. As with many old towns, the decorative elevation at the front faces the street, while the side and back elevations are simple.

According to Blenheim's chief executive Dominic Hare, Woodstock's vitality – which will partly depend on the right housing provision – is essential to the interests of the estate. 'Blenheim is super aligned to the place it's in. For the estate to flourish, it's essential that the area around it is flourishing.' Unlike other businesses, a landed estate can't pick itself up and move somewhere else. Equally, the success of the towns and villages around Blenheim depends in large measure on the estate, which is 'an economic pillar of the area.' Woodstock's fortunes have always been linked to those of Blenheim Palace: in previous centuries, local trades included glove-making and the fabrication of cut-steel ornaments, trade for which came from the visitors to Vanbrugh's masterpiece. Although the town bustled into the late-20th century with good local shops and numerous pubs, some family businesses have closed in recent years. One factor in the decline has been the difficulty of finding local staff in an area where the cost of living is so high.

Not everyone in Woodstock embraces a vision involving such a dramatic expansion of the town, but the District Council, aware of Oxfordshire's requirement to find one hundred thousand new homes by 2031 under the Strategic Housing Market Assessment, is supportive. The emerging West Oxfordshire and Cherwell Local Plans include four development sites on Blenheim estate land. Doubters should be reassured by the architectural ambition already evident at Park View where the principles are the same as Nansledan, but translated into the vernacular of the east Cotswolds: no home will be more than a few minutes from the local shops; there will be no visible difference between affordable and open market housing; car speeds are controlled by the way the streets are laid out; and local materials are used where possible. Houses are built from a varied palette of materials. Some have roofs of carefully chosen and graded artificial stone slate, as well as porches from a range, inspired by the Georgian architect James Gibbs, which Hugh has designed for Haddonstone. As at Nansledan, the more prominent houses have been finished more expensively, because these are the ones that catch the eye. Some are of odd shapes, as though they had been fitted to sites created by historical accident, of the kind often seen in old towns.

When finished, Park View will form a semi-independent hamlet, based around a square. There will be commercial premises, 'so that residents will have the hugely attractive option of being able to work around the corner from where they live.' The workspaces will appeal to people starting new businesses, including the growing band of 'late life entrepreneurs.' One benefit, for those approaching Woodstock from the east, is that it will shield an unsightly 1960s housing estate laid out around cul-de-sacs. By contrast, Hugh's architecture will be appropriate to Woodstock's Georgian core. A high discount is offered on all affordable rental – up to 40% off the market value. 'We want families to keep together, and not be split for economic reasons,' says Mr Hare.

There will be an obelisk on one corner of the square by the main road, the plinth of which will be embellished by a young stone carver. This will be the happy fulfilment of a planning obligation that required the developers to provide an element of public art, which happened to arise at the time of the Grinling Gibbons Festival celebrating the tercentenary of the great carver's death. As a member of the Carpenters' Company, Hugh was on the Festival steering group of interested Livery Companies in the City of London. Since Gibbons was responsible for some of the carving at Blenheim Palace, it seemed appropriate to embrace the connection. The winners of a competition for young carvers run as part of the Gibbons Festival will be asked to submit ideas for an original piece of work to celebrate the Estate's commitment to improving sustainability and ecology. In this way the Park View commission will help launch the career of two young carvers, whilst providing the

development with an exemplary piece of original public art. This virtuous circle is the latest of a number of such projects that Hugh has succeeded in bringing to fruition over the years.

Blenheim is not the only estate to be following the Duchy of Cornwall's example at Poundbury and Nansledan. Encouraged by The Prince's Foundation, it has become part of a movement that is being called Landowner Legacy. Landowners not only have an opportunity to profit from the demand for new housing, but local authorities, anxious to meet the housing targets set for them by central government, are eager that they should build. Equally, as at Blenheim, it is important to the well-being of the estate that the quality of the development should be as high as possible: owners know that their heirs' successors will have to live with the consequences for as long as the family is there. Simply selling plots to volume house builders for short term gain will produce a visually unsatisfactory result which does nothing for the cohesiveness of the estate; nor will it ultimately make as great an economic return as a long-term approach.

Above: Stone-fronted buildings at the edge of Park View.

Right: A street in the middle of the scheme, showing lime-rendered walls and slate or tile roofs. The technical term for the Cotswold stones set on their edges on the top of the garden wall is cock and hen capping.

Left: An example of the variety of the building materials at Park View.

Above: The edge of the scheme. These houses are looking onto permanent green space: it is the protected site of the remains of a Roman villa, one of many around the Cotswolds.

Landowner Legacy has caught on. Meetings to discuss what it could mean for individual landowners have attracted audiences of well over a hundred. With so much interest, master-planning of such developments has become something of a speciality for Hugh. Other clients include Burghley House, Lincolnshire, where a two thousand-home development is in prospect, partly on Burghley land; and the Hon. Timothy Knatchbull, grandson of Lord Mountbatten, who is pursuing a major development on land that he inherited at Ashfield, part of the Broadlands estate in Hampshire.

Right: Aerial CGI view of the completed scheme. The left hand side of the scheme has already been built, while the rest is developing. The main square with its obelisk is visible in the centre.

MASTERPLANNING & URBAN DESIGN

THE DUCHY OF CORNWALL ESTATE
KENNINGTON

The Duchy of Cornwall has owned the manor of Kennington since it was created for the Black Prince in 1337. This makes it the oldest of the great London estates, and it remains among a handful that is still traditionally managed. As the Duchy's consultant architect at Kennington, Hugh considers the urban fabric – how to maintain the character of a place that has been managed with unusual care by successive Princes of Wales; and how to introduce the subtle improvements in streetscape that not only look good but contribute to social well-being. These interventions can be at the micro level: redeveloping an ugly row of garages around which undesirable activities had been taking place for example. They also concern a large sports venue which is one of the landmarks of British life.

THE OVAL

The Surrey Cricket Club is not as old as the Duchy of Cornwall, but since its foundation in 1845 it has always played at the Oval. Previously, the land had been used as market gardens which had been surrounded by an oval of road in about 1790. By the end of the 19th century, the ground had been equipped with a pavilion and stands, in the jaunty style of Victorian sporting architecture, surmounted by two brick towers. When the entrance front was raised in the 1970s, these towers were kept in an act of homage to the club's history. But other changes were less benign. Turnstiles and cabins at the south end kept the public at bay, and not only on match days. In an area of London that has not always been prosperous, the Oval got a reputation for being aloof from its neighbours – a preserve of toffs. The backs of the stands created dark and cavernous spaces that were a magnet for nefarious goings-on. The site called for a masterplan of its own, which would restore a sense of arrival for cricket lovers and stitch this important asset back into the community that surrounded it.

The turnstiles went. Here, technology helped since it is now easy for club staff to scan tickets using hand-held devices. Hugh took gates designed by Louis de Soissons, a previous Duchy architect, as the inspiration for new wrought-iron railings and gates that give passers-by an unobstructed view of the entrance. That entrance, formerly obscured by lurid advertising displays and other clutter, has now been reimagined. It is marked by a tetrastyle portico in antis (four columns that stand within the enclosure formed by two solid bays), whose capitals are decorated with ostrich feathers derived from the badge of The Prince of Wales, which is also the badge of the Surrey Cricket Club. Above the cornice are two cheeky urns that look remarkably like a larger version of those in which the Ashes, sacred to England-Australia Tests, rest: for the original match which led to the burning of the stumps was not played at Lord's (sorry, MCC) but at the Oval. Tradition, in the upper echelons of cricket, is all important, and Hugh was at pains to respect the form of the old buildings in his remodelling. Cornice line and string courses are at the same height and of the same material (Bath Stone) as those that already existed. The handmade orange brick (from what became a bespoke Oval Blend from E.H. Smith), laid in wide bands of lime mortar, sparkle in the sunshine that (in imagination) invariably greets the arriving crowd. Inside, key entertainment spaces such as The Prince of Wales Room have been made bigger, while the seating capacity of the stands as a whole has been doubled in size.

The masterplan envisages the Oval becoming a 'modern Colosseum'. The execution and detail of the vision has been left to Rolfe Judd, specialists in the architecture of sports clubs. One of the considerations has been to create sheltered spaces where the crowd can mingle during those times (not, to be realistic, unknown) when rain stops play. The detailing is in a somewhat Art Deco style that marries Modernism and Classicism. Since Surrey Cricket Club began life in a tavern called The Horns (demolished in the 1960s), it is appropriate that, in a major initiative, they have, for the first time in their history, acquired land outside the confines of the Oval on which to build a hotel. Another hotel is being created, although not by the club, out of the famous Victorian gasometer adjacent to the boundary wall to the east.

Previous spread: Portico of The Oval cricket ground: the ostrich feathers in the capitals acknowledge that the ground-landlord is the Duchy of Cornwall. They are also the cricket club badge.

Left: Archways on the first floor show the quality of the brickwork.

THE WIDER ESTATE

Although a significant amount of the Duchy estate at Kennington has been sold over the past thirty years, it still retains a number of sites. Hugh's task has been to advise on ways in which the quality of the building stock can be raised to improve the area. Fortunately, previous Princes of Wales have been as conscientious in their approach to the architecture of this part of London as the most recent holders of the title. At the beginning of the 20th century, the Duchy employed the firm of Adshead & Ramsey to build new terraces, squares and public buildings in a light and urbane style, with sash windows and shallow classical detail; beautifully laid brickwork combined elegance with economy. This firm was succeeded in the inter-war period by Louis de Soissons, architect-planner of Welwyn Garden City, an architect of wide tastes that included the Regency. Not everything, however, is of the standard set by these champions of tradition and some of the housing put up in the aftermath of the Second World War is cheaply built and poorly conceived. It is now time for it to come down. Fortunately, because fairly large areas of street and terrace are in one ownership, rebuilding gives an opportunity to plan them better.

Right: Bricks laid in English bond were matched to the buildings either side. Everything in Hugh's design does its best to fit in with what was already there.

Renovation of a block of nurses' flats could give the opportunity to create a community garden. A former county court building, designed in the stripped-down Classical style of the mid-20th century and now listed grade 2, could be repurposed for a combination of residential and commercial units without destroying the architecture of the court rooms. Buildings on what must once have been a mews, to judge from the name of Stables Way, could be rebuilt in conjunction with St Anselm's Church which owns the adjacent site. This could not only provide some badly needed homes, but would eliminate the sort of poorly lit and little supervised locale where anti-social behaviour has been known to take place. These are all planning proposals which Hugh has advanced after consultation with Lambeth Borough Council. The schemes may not actually be designed by him. His hand can, however, be seen at 91 Kennington Lane whose site had previously been home to a scruffy collection of garages that were used as much for storage as keeping cars. Hugh produced a handsome scheme in the late Georgian style of nearby streets, with doorcase, sash windows and walls of traditional yellow stock brick. Once the design had been made and planning permission achieved, the site was sold to be built out by TLS Investments Ltd.

Above: (Top left) Details of the ostrich feather capitals designed by Charlie Gurrey, formerly Dick Reid's assistant. (Top right) Stairway, showing brickwork and stone copings.

GROUND FLOOR

KEY
A   Lift

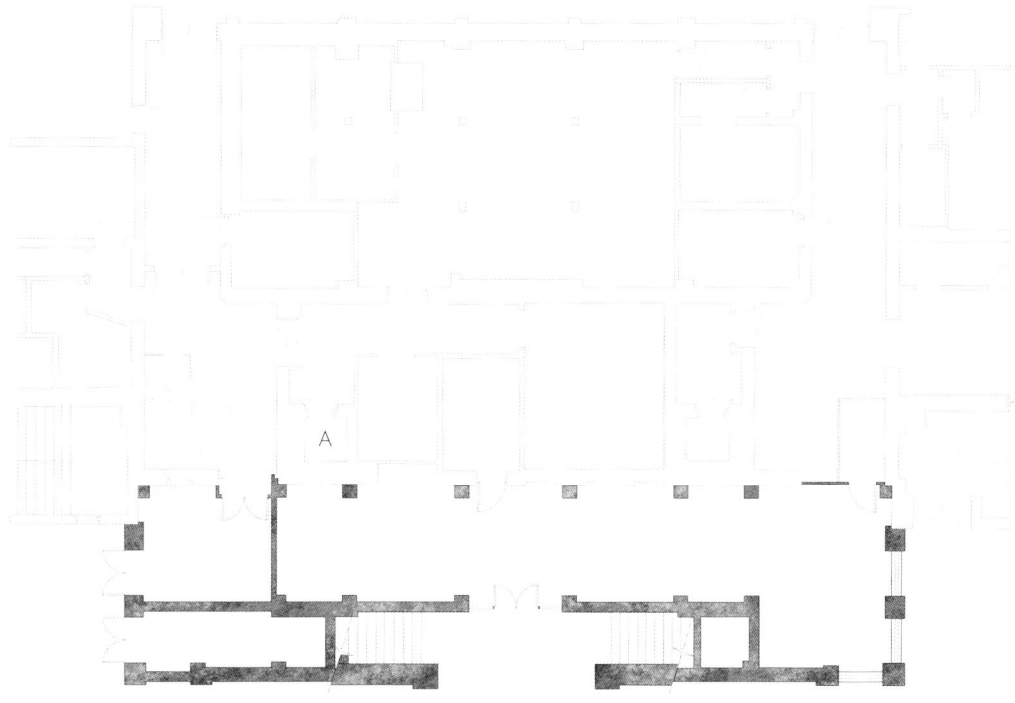

FIRST FLOOR

KEY
A   Members' Bar
B   Members' Terrace

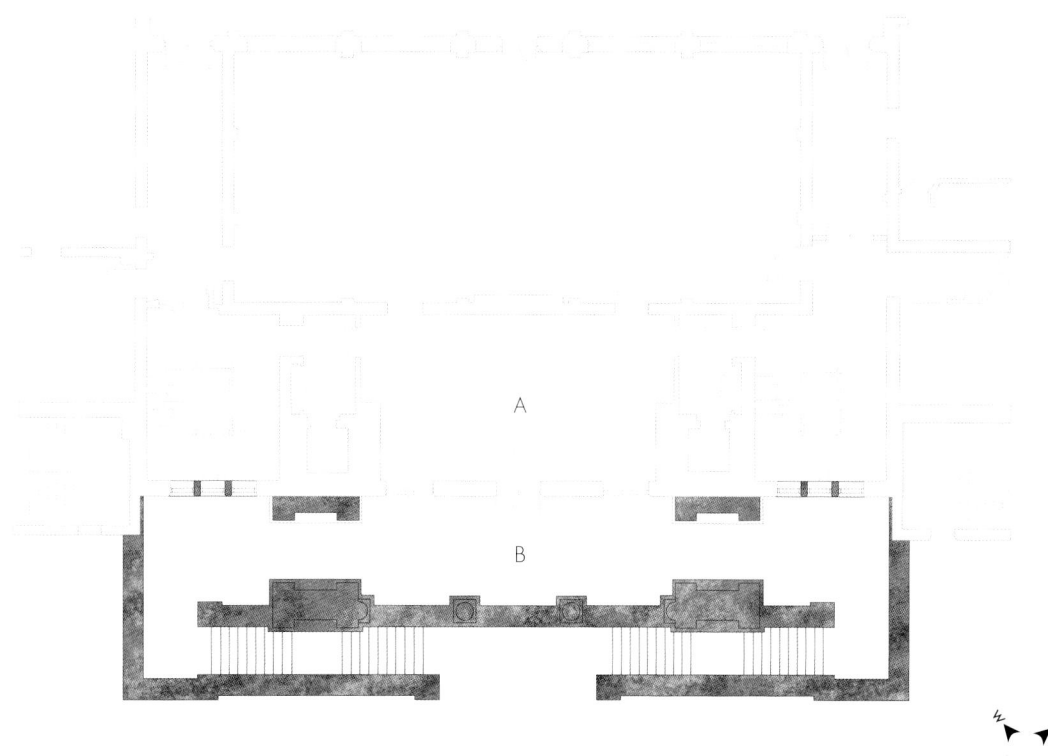

Sweeping new buildings by Rolfe Judd fulfill Hugh's masterplan in an Art Deco idiom.

Details of the windows and the panels in the cornice above.

Hobbs gate, suavely designed by a previous Duchy of Cornwall architect, Louis de Soissons and repositioned by Hugh into a more appropriate central location.

Three watercolours by Chris Draper show the evolution of the masterplan: here, before the arrival of the new buildings.

Entry is now through the new portico and the blocks on the right, designed by Rolfe Judd, are shown in relation to the rest of Kennington.

Above: Vision for the completed Colosseum, with Art Deco blocks enclosing The Oval ground in a manner that both brings greater harmony to surrounding streets and more income to the Surrey Cricket Club.

Right: Showing seating and the layout of the club. The symmetry of the plan has been improved by Hugh working in concert with Rolfe Judd Architects.

HUGH PETTER

SEEING POTENTIAL

One of the great thrills for any architect is visiting a new site, meeting a new client, taking their brief and engaging the brain. Whether it is altering and extending an existing building, a replacement building, a new building on a virgin site, or an urban development, there is nothing to match that initial excitement and stimulation. With any client I try to listen very carefully to understand their needs, make comments and suggestions where I feel it necessary to help them make good decisions, but always respecting that this is their project not mine.

Above: Early sketch of Stanton Farm, on scrap paper, in Hugh's favourite brown ink.

My job, as architect, is to add value through good design, not just to impose my own will. Quite often we will look initially at alternative ideas so that the client can make a positive decision as to which option suits them best. I like to draw in pencil, sometimes freehand on graph paper, so it is spontaneous and not precious or polished to help encourage my clients to engage actively in the process.

It is vital at the outset to understand any constraints: to a good architect they are stimulants to create more satisfactory outcomes. With a listed building this means understanding the history and evolution of the structure and the relative importance of each phase of work. Such an understanding creates a solid framework into which one can begin to weave ideas, safe in the knowledge that, in due course, one will have the necessary arguments to hand to explain the scheme convincingly to the heritage authorities. For me, history is a living phenomenon, and I see my work as the latest phase of an ongoing pattern of change, often using the same architectural character as the earlier building so that it all fits together beautifully. There is no need to be self-consciously different because, like handwriting and prose, the work of every architect is inevitably unique and the aesthetic harmony of the whole matters more than the ego of the individual.

As we all become more aware of sustainability we perhaps try a bit harder to reuse existing buildings rather than just flatten them and start again. An ability to look and understand the various previous phases of alteration is helpful, so looking beyond a current muddle to the jewel that may be lurking beneath. You need survey plans too to understand the structure, to plan the flow, to ensure good proportions and to balance the scale of the accommodation in each part of the plan. Survey elevations too are vital to sketch over. Sometimes it takes several attempts to boil down a design: each time it is drawn it gets better! As many famous writers have observed:

"If I had more time I would have written you a shorter letter."

Buildings must always be seen in their settings. How a country house relates to its garden and wider landscape, and how a new college building relates to the older buildings – not only in terms of style and materials but in the forming of new quads and garden areas – are all matters of vital importance. Similarly how an urban development links to the old town, to the wider landscape, and how one can leave road tails that future phases of development can graft onto to make a permeable network that is attractive for pedestrians and cyclists are all points which are fundamental to success.

Before cheap fossil fuels, vernacular buildings and old towns were intrinsically sustainable because they could not have the luxury of being otherwise. So there is much to learn from the past to help inform the future.

Follow these principles and there is every chance that a new design will feel 'right', heft in its time and place, sustainable, and well attuned to a client's needs.

Hugh Petter
Winchester
September 2022

THE OVAL: The mission was to create a new front on what was originally the back of the pavilion. The existing bands of stone, towers and so on provided a framework onto which one could add a portico using the same materials and proportions, embellished with appropriate detail.

STANTON FARM: Makes the most of a glorious site that was ignored by the previous house, and locks on to the existing range of barn buildings in the Palladian manner.

SAWMILL COTTAGE: Develops the romantic character intended in the earlier house of a gingerbread house in the woods.

IVY COTTAGE, HAMPSHIRE: A long, one-room thick, 'single pile' plan cottage from the 1730s. Hugh added a new family kitchen and more bedrooms to the rear with cross gable roofs in the traditional manner. All materials and details match as closely as possible those of the original building with a blend of three bricks laid in Flemish bond in lime mortar, a clay tile roof, and bespoke joinery.

FAWLER MANOR: A good example of 'instant history' – the new wing, with large sash windows is conceptually a late 18th-century addition to an earlier manor done in a way which is at once familiar to us all, and where the new enlarged building still enjoys a coherent underlying structure and palette of materials.

A HOUSE IN HAMPSHIRE: A large and beautiful site which had developed incrementally but without regard to the coherence and convenience of the whole, and where the building was not properly 'locked' into its setting. The original cottage became the 'service wing' to the new main house extension.

CATALOGUE RAISONNÉ

KEY
A   Alterations
E   Extensions
R   Repairs
RH Replacement House
NB New Build
CHD Commercial Housing Development
MP Masterplan

The following catalogue showcases the work of Hugh Petter from 1994 to the present day. A longstanding director at ADAM Architecture, Hugh's work is strongly influenced by classicism. His practice draws from Vignola, Palladio and Gibbs, but also from the Arts and Crafts movement, and respect for traditional materials and craftsmanship is paramount in his work.

2022
UPHAM, HAMPSHIRE
Upham House
A, R

2021
WEST MEON, HAMPSHIRE
Lippen Wood Farm
A, E

2021
MYLOR CHURCHTOWN, CORNWALL
Porloe Farm
A, E

2021
LONG CRENDON, BUCKINGHAMSHIRE
Sandy Lane
CHD

2021
WOODBURY, DEVON
Globe Hill
CHD

2021
WARNHAM, WEST SUSSEX
Freeman Road
MP, CHD

2021
FRENSHAM, SURREY
Frensham Manor and outbuildings
A, E

2021
BRAMDEAN, HAMPSHIRE
Woodcote Manor
A, E

2020
EAST SOMERTON, NORFOLK
Pool House and Orangery, Burnley Hall
NB

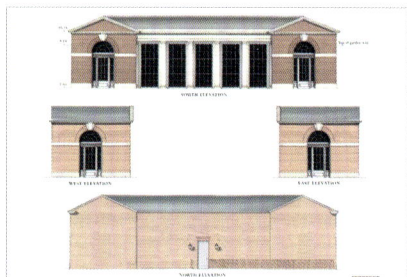

2020
PRESTON CANDOVER, HAMPSHIRE
North Hall
A, E

2020
HELFORD PASSAGE, CORNWALL
Penmorva
RH

2020
DEWLISH, DORSET
Dewlish House
A, E, R

2020
PUCKSHIPTON, WILTSHIRE
Puckshipton House
A, E, R

2020
SWANMORE, HAMPSHIRE
Hill Place
A, E, R

2020
UPHAM, HAMPSHIRE
Commercial Units and Holiday Cottage, Newlyn's Farm
NB

2019
STAMFORD, LINCOLNSHIRE
St Martins Park
MP, CHD

2019
PETWORTH, WEST SUSSEX
CHD

2019
NORTH BADDESLEY, HAMPSHIRE
Hoe Lane
CHD

2019
HOUGHTON DOWN, HAMPSHIRE
Merlins
RH

2018
SANDRINGHAM, NORFOLK
CHD

2018
ST MARTIN, JERSEY
Seymour Farm
RH

2018
ACTON TURVILLE, GLOUCESTERSHIRE
MP, CHD

2018
GUNTON, NORFOLK
Steward's House, Gunton Park
NB

2017
BARNHAM BROOM, NORFOLK
Dades Farm
A, E

2017
UPHAM, HAMPSHIRE
Newlyn's Farm
A, E

2017
KENNINGTON, LONDON
Court House
A, E

2017
HUNGERFORD, BERKSHIRE
Leverton Manor
RH

2017
ODIHAM, HAMPSHIRE
The Priory
A, E

2017
TRINITY, JERSEY
Meadow Farm
A, E

2017
BLANDFORD FORUM, DORSET
Stour House
A, R

2017
ROMSEY, HAMPSHIRE
Luzborough
CHD

2016
SHOTESHAM ST MARY, NORFOLK
Park Farm House
A, E

2016
PRESTON CANDOVER, HAMPSHIRE
Old Timbers
A, E

2016
CHANNEL ISLANDS
RH

2016
GUNTON, NORFOLK
Boathouse, Gunton Park
NB

2016
PHILADELPHIA, USA
Linden Hill
MP, CHD

2016
THURSLEY, SURREY
Hill House Farm Barns
NB

2016
CHICHESTER, WEST SUSSEX
Graylingwell
CHD

2016
KINGS NYMPTON, DEVON
King's Nympton Park
A, R

2015
WEST WOODHAY, BERKSHIRE
The Cottage, The Old Rectory
A, R

2015
WOODSTOCK, OXFORDSHIRE
Park View
MP
Estates Gazette Award 2021: Approach to affordable housing
Housebuilder Award 2020

CATALOGUE RAISONNÉ

2015
KENNINGTON, LONDON
60 and 65 Sancroft Street
NB

2015
CHETTLE, DORSET
Chettle House
A, R
The Georgian Group Awards 2019: Restoration of a Georgian country house

2015
CHETTLE, DORSET
Pool House and Garage, Chettle House
NB
The Georgian Group Awards 2019: Restoration of a Georgian country house

2015
SWAINES HILL, HAMPSHIRE
High Beeches
RH

2015
ROPLEY, HAMPSHIRE
Ropley House
A, E

2015
ASH GREEN, SURREY
Warren Farm
MP, CHD

2015
PRIVETT, HAMPSHIRE
Church Farm House
A, E

2015
COBHAM, SURREY
2 Burstead Close
RH

2015
COBHAM, SURREY
3 Oxshott Rise
RH

2015
WEST MEON, HAMPSHIRE
Hall Place
A, E

2014
LONG HANBOROUGH, OXFORDSHIRE
MP, CHD

2014
BROWN CANDOVER, HAMPSHIRE
Manor Farm
A, E

2014
COBHAM, SURREY
21 Broad Highway
RH

2014
OWSLEBURY, HAMPSHIRE
Great Hunts Place
A, E

2014
BUCKLER'S HARD, HAMPSHIRE
Mariners' Quay
A, E

2014
OXSHOTT, SURREY
15 Princes Drive
RH

2014
COBHAM, SURREY
11 Eaton Park
RH

2014
STAMFORD, LINCOLNSHIRE
Stamford North Urban Extension
MP

2014
BENTWORTH, HAMPSHIRE
Childer Hill Farm
A, E

2014
ESHER, SURREY
Residential Project
A, E

2013
HEADLEY, BERKSHIRE
Headley Stud
RH

2013
WESTHAMPNETT, WEST SUSSEX
Stane Street
CHD

2013
BRAMDEAN, HAMPSHIRE
The Gomms
A, E

2013
ALRESFORD, HAMPSHIRE
45 Broad Street
A, E, R

2013
WOOTTON ST LAWRENCE, HAMPSHIRE
Tangier House
A, E

2013
BRAMDEAN, HAMPSHIRE
Woodcote Manor
A, E, R

2013
RAMSBURY, WILTSHIRE
Scrope House
A, E

2013
UPPER FARRINGDON, HAMPSHIRE
Manor House
A, E

2013
BROUGHTON, HAMPSHIRE
School Lane
MP, CHD

2013
BEAUWORTH, HAMPSHIRE
Beauworth Manor
A, E

2013
COBHAM, SURREY
17 Harebell Hill
RH

2013
HAMPSHIRE
Ivy Cottage
A, E

2013
TRURO, CORNWALL
Tregavethan Manor
RH

2012
STEVENTON, HAMPSHIRE
Orchard House
A, E

2012
FAWLER, OXFORDSHIRE
Fawler Manor
A, E, R

2012
SPARSHOLT, HAMPSHIRE
The Maples
RH

2012
THURSLEY, SURREY
Haybarn
RH

2012
STEVENTON, HAMPSHIRE
Steventon Manor
A, E

2012
HAMPSHIRE
A House in Hampshire
A, E

2012
SWAINS HILL, HAMPSHIRE
High Beeches
RH

2012
Haddonstone: The GIBBS Range of Classical Porches
NB

2011
ROPLEY, HAMPSHIRE
Ropley House
A, E, R

2011
HAMBLEDON, HAMPSHIRE
Fairfield House
A, E
2011

MAYFAIR, LONDON
6 Farm Street
A, E

2011
PRIVETT, HAMPSHIRE
Hurst Farm
A, E

2011
NEWTON VALENCE, HAMPSHIRE
Inadown House
A, E

2011
UPHAM, HAMPSHIRE
Shoot Dining Room, The Holt
A

2010
EAST MOLESEY, LONDON
Arragon House
A

2010
BROUGHTON, HAMPSHIRE
Orchard House
A, E

2010
COBO, GUERNSEY
Les Carterets
NB

CATALOGUE RAISONNÉ

2010
EAST MOLESEY, LONDON
Prestbury House
A, E

2010
BARTON STACEY, HAMPSHIRE
The Old Vicarage
A, E

2010
PANGBOURNE, BERKSHIRE
Farm Cottage
A, E

2010
PANGBOURNE, BERKSHIRE
Bere Court Farm
RH

2010
LOWER SWELL, GLOUCESTERSHIRE
Fayrefields
RH

2010
BRANSBURY, HAMPSHIRE
The Old Dairy
A, E

2010
KENNINGTON CROSS, LONDON
St Anselm's Church
NB

2010
KENNINGTON, LONDON
Arora Hotel
NB

2010
SOUTH CHERITON, SOMERSET
Woodside
RH

2010
WINDLESHAM, SURREY
Half Moon House
A, E

2010
KENNINGTON, LONDON
95-97 Kennington Lane
NB

2010
HUISH, WILTSHIRE
The Old Rectory
A, E

2009
TRINITY COLLEGE, OXFORD
The Levine Building
NB
Georgian Group Awards 2022: Best New Building in a Georgian Context
Oxford Preservation Trust Awards 2022: Recogising the Contribution to Oxford

2009
BROADWELL, GLOUCESTERSHIRE
Outbuilding, Fieldside House
NB

2009
HAMMERSMITH, LONDON
16 Hammersmith Terrace
A, E

2009
RICHMOND, LONDON
20 & 21-22 The Green
A, E

2009
ITCHEN ABBAS, HAMPSHIRE
Itchen Down House
A, E

2009
KENNINGTON, LONDON
Hansom Mews
NB

2009
ST HELIER, JERSEY
Westwater
NB

2008
KNOWLE, WARWICKSHIRE
Batts Hall
RH
Marvin Architect's Challenge Award 2013: New house in Warwickshire

2008
HARE HATCH, BERKSHIRE
Bear Ash
RH

2008
TILFORD, SURREY
Monksfield
RH

2008
BRINKLEY, CAMBRIDGESHIRE
Brinkley Hall
A, E

2008
AWBRIDGE, HAMPSHIRE
Awbridge House Farm
RH

2008
UPTON GREY, HAMPSHIRE
The Dower House
A, E

2008
WEST WOODHAY, BERKSHIRE
The Old Rectory
A, E, R

2008
SEVENOAKS, KENT
117 Kippington Road
RH

2007
NEWQUAY, CORNWALL
Tregunnel Hill
MP, CHD
UK Property Awards 2018:
Residential Development
INTBAU Excellence Award 2018:
Urban Design
Planning Award 2018: High Commendation
Congress for the New Urbanism (CNU)
Charter Award 2018

2007
BEER, DEVON
York House
A, E

2007
ASPLEY GUISE, BEDFORDSHIRE
Woodcote
NB

2007
MOULTON, CAMBRIDGESHIRE
Moulton Stud
NB

2007
OCKHAM, SURREY
Blackmoor Farm
RH

2007
BELGRAVIA, LONDON
32 Eaton Place
A, E

2007
KENNINGTON, LONDON
Duchy of Cornwall
MP

2007
CHERITON, HAMPSHIRE
The Old Rectory
A, E

2006
STOKE, HAMPSHIRE
Grove House
RH

2006
YARMOUTH, ISLE OF WIGHT
Shandon
A, E

2006
ALDBURY, HERTFORDSHIRE
Stocks Golf Club
NB

2006
WEST MEON, HAMPSHIRE
Lippen Wood Farm
A, E

2006
UPTON GREY, HAMPSHIRE
Old Barn House
A, E

2006
SWAINES HILL, HAMPSHIRE
Swaines Hill Manor
A, E

2006
KINETON, WARWICKSHIRE
Longbourn Farm
RH

2006
ALRESFORD, HAMPSHIRE
The Pink House
A, E

2006
CLAPHAM, LONDON
House on Clapham Common
A, E
RIBA Competition to renovate and extend Grade II Listed house 2006: Winner

2005
CO. KILDARE, EIRE
Barretstown
NB

2005
UPHAM, HAMPSHIRE
The Holt
A, E

2005
FARRINGDON, HAMPSHIRE
Upper Woodside Cottage
A, E

2005
FARRINGDON, HAMPSHIRE
Upper Woodside House
A, E

2004
KENNINGTON, LONDON
The Oval
MP, E
UK Property Awards 2015: Best Leisure Architecture, London
Congress for the New Urbanism (CNU) Charter Awards 2015: Merit Award

RICS (Royal Institute of Chartered Surveyors) London Awards 2015: Tourism & Leisure category, Highly Commended
Brick Awards Shortlist 2014: Best Commercial Building and Best Craftsmanship
The Georgian Group Awards 2013: New Building in the Classical Tradition, Commended

2004
HERRIARD, HAMPSHIRE
Elderfield House and Cottage
A, E

2004
HAMBLEDON, SURREY
Court Farm
A, E

2004
OWSLEBURY, HAMPSHIRE
Great Hunts Place
A, E

2004
WEST VIRGINIA, USA
Homestead Preserve
NB

2004
NORTHAW, HERTFORDSHIRE
West Lodge, Northaw House
RH

2004
STANTON ST BERNARD, WILTSHIRE
Stanton Farm
RH

2004
SHAWFORD, HAMPSHIRE
Lane House
A, E

2004
HAMBLEDON, HAMPSHIRE
West End House
A, E

2004
BERKSHIRE
A Stone House outside London
RH

2004
EAST WOODHAY, BERKSHIRE
Moongrove
RH

2004
DROXFORD, HAMPSHIRE
Fir Hill
A, E

2004
ALDBURY, HERTFORDSHIRE
Stocks House
A, E

2004
KILMACOLM, SCOTLAND
Avenel
NB
Herald Property Awards 2012: Best Luxury Home presented to Scops Development, new Arts & Crafts house (Plot 2)
UK Property Awards 2011: Best Architecture (Single Unit), new Arts & Crafts house (Plot 3), Highly Commended
Herald Property Awards 2011: Best Luxury Home presented to Scops Development, new Arts & Crafts house (Plot 3)
Herald Property Awards 2009: Best Luxury Home presented to Scops Development, new Arts & Crafts house (Plot 1)

2003
RAMRIDGE, HAMPSHIRE
Ramridge Garden Cottage
RH

2003
BRAMDEAN, HAMPSHIRE
Bramdean Farm House
A, E

2003
TIMSBURY, HAMPSHIRE
Herons Mead
RH

2003
ESHER, SURREY
Pennyfarthing
NB

2003
OWSLEBURY, HAMPSHIRE
Marwell Farm
A, E

2003
LAVERTON, NORTH YORKSHIRE
Sawmill Cottage
A, E

2003
NEWQUAY, CORNWALL
Nansledan
MP, CHD
National Urban Design Award 2021
AJ Architecture Awards 2021: Highly Commended
RIBA South West Regional Award 2021
Planning Awards 2021: Shortlist
South West Residential Property Awards 2021: Shortlist for Large Residential Development of the Year
Civic Trust Award 2020: Regional Finalist for Phase 1
British Homes Award 2020: Highly Commended
UK Property Awards 2019: Architecture Multiple Residence
International Making Cities Livable (IMCL) 'Selected for Exhibition' Award 2015: Designing for Green, Healthy Cities

2003
CUDDINGTON, BUCKINGHAMSHIRE
Lower Farm
A, E (with Kathryn Findlay)

2003
CHILWORTH, SURREY
Powder Mills Cottage
A, E

2003
HAMMERSMITH, LONDON
15 Hammersmith Terrace
A, E

2003
ST JAMES'S, LONDON
196a Piccadilly
A, E

2003
THURSLEY, SURREY
Sunset Cottage
A, E

2003
HAMPTON WICK, LONDON
Moiravale
NB

2003
WASHINGTON DC, USA
The Cox House
A, E

2003
ATLANTA, USA
Millennium Gate
NB
McGraw-Hill Southeast Construction Award 2006: Best Public Building Award
Palladio Award 2006

2003
GUILDFORD, SURREY
Warwicks Bench
RH

2003
BEAUWORTH, HAMPSHIRE
Jackdaws
A, E

2003
MALTON, NORTH YORKSHIRE
Settrington House
A, E

2003
MAYFAIR, LONDON
21-23 Farm Street
NB

2003
CHELSEA, LONDON
35 Tedworth Square
A, E

2003
BRAMLEY, SURREY
The Lodge, Snowdenham Hall
A, E

2003
PARADISE ISLAND, THE BAHAMAS
Pembroke House
NB

2003
ASCOT, BERKSHIRE
Fox Hollow
A, E

2003
HAMPSTEAD, LONDON
20 Ellerdale Road
A, E

2003
CHILTON CANDOVER, HAMPSHIRE
Bugmore Cottages
A, E

2003
ISINGTON, HAMPSHIRE
Isington Mill
A, E

2003
CHILTON CANDOVER, HAMPSHIRE
Bugmore Hill
RH

2003
BELGRAVIA, LONDON
33 Hans Place
A, E

2003
NOTTING HILL, LONDON
17 Northumberland Place
A, E

2003
BEAUWORTH, HAMPSHIRE
Shorley Wood
A, E

2003
EWHURST, SURREY
Marylands
A, E

2003
BRENTFORD, MIDDLESEX
Boat House and Fishery Pavilion, Syon Park
NB

2003
WINCHESTER, HAMPSHIRE
Minster House
A, E, R

2003
THURSLEY, SURREY
Hill House Farm
RH

2003
GRANGE OVER SANDS, CUMBRIA
Holker Hall
MP

2003
UPPER FARRINGDON, HAMPSHIRE
Manor House
A, E

2003
SYDLING ST NICHOLAS, DORSET
Up Sydling
A, E

2003
CHELTENHAM, GLOUCESTERSHIRE
45 The Park
RH
Daily Mail UK Property Awards, 2008, Five Star Award for Best Architecture (Single Unit) UK Commended Cheltenham Civic Trust Award, 2008 The Georgian Group Giles Worsley Award for a New Building in a Georgian Context, 2007

2003
CHENIES, BUCKINGHAMSHIRE
Chenies House
RH

2003
ROME, ITALY
The British School at Rome
A, E

1999
WANDSWORTH, LONDON
44 Bucharest Road
A, E

1999
IBSTONE, BUCKINGHAMSHIRE
Grays
A, E

1999
MAYFAIR, LONDON
105 Mount Street
A, E

1999
ORPINGTON, KENT
1 Birchwood Road
A, E

1999
PITCH HILL, EWHURST
Copse Hill
A, E

1998
BELGRAVIA, LONDON
18 Wilton Place
A, E

1998
WIMBLEDON, LONDON
97 Arthur Road
A, E

1998
ROCHFORD, ESSEX
New Hall
A, E
Civic Trust and North Yorkshire RIBA
Harrogate District Award for Environmental
Excellence 1998: Commendation

1997
RICHMOND, LONDON
1 Maids of Honour Row
A, R

1997
JEWELLERY QUARTER, BIRMINGHAM
Information Kiosk
NB

1995
DOUGHTON, GLOUCESTERSHIRE
Pump House, Highgrove
NB

1995
MERTON, LONDON
Wandle Villa
A, E

1995
TEDDINGTON, LONDON
11 Oxford Road
A, E

1994
PUTNEY, LONDON
20 Gwendolen Avenue
A, E

1994
ROMSEY, HAMPSHIRE
Farley Semaphore
A, E

1994
HAMPSTEAD, LONDON
30 Crediton Hill
A, E

1994
NORTH YORKSHIRE
Birstwith Hall, Nr Harrogate
A, E
Commendation Civic Trust and North Yorkshire
RIBA Harrogate District Award for Environmental
Excellence 1998, Birstwith Hall, Harrogate

CATALOGUE RAISONNÉ

The staff at ADAM Architecture outside their office in Winchester.

ACKNOWLEDGEMENTS

"There will never be great architects or great architecture without great patrons" – so said one of my architecture heroes, Sir Edwin Lutyens. For my own part, I have enjoyed indecent luck with the clients I have had the good fortune to work with so far in my career. The opportunities have been exhilarating; the collaboration has almost invariably been stimulating and enjoyable, and many of the friendships forged over the course of a project have endured long after the last tradesman has left site. My heartfelt thanks to them all.

Thanks too are due to my current director colleagues at ADAM Architecture, Nigel Anderson, George Saumarez Smith, Robbie Kerr, Darren Price and Robert Cox, and to my ex-director colleagues Robert Adam and Paul Hanvey. The older members of this group nurtured me generously in my youth and have supported me thereafter, not least in producing this handsome book. In turn I hope I can offer similar support to those that come after me. We are fortunate too in being supported by an extraordinarily able and committed team of people, without whom none of the projects in these pages could have been produced. In particular I should mention Ian Aburrow, Cory Babb, Sue Beaumont, Helen Lawrence Beaton, Ben Bolgar, Steve Bushell, Fredrik Carlsson, Peter Critoph, Wayne Derrick, Nigel Gilkison, Sharron Harman, Mark Hoare, Jenn Holmes, Pedro Honwana, Shaun Knight, Ian Lawrence, Victor Man, Alex Montague Smith, Paul Pizzo and Wayne Reakes. We could not ask for a better or nicer group of people around us. I must offer especial thanks too to Claire Groves, my PA for over 15 years. She has worked hard with me on many of the projects that appear in these pages, and to weave the threads of this book together. Thanks are due also to Delia Edwards who has worked so hard to help with the later stages of this project.

Architectural and Urban Design projects are, by their very nature, a group activity and the list of consultants, contractors, local authority officers with whom I have collaborated during my career would fill another book of this size. The vast majority have been a joy to work with and have enriched the projects that we have worked on together in so many ways. I offer my thanks to them all.

It has been such fun to revisit old projects with my old friend Clive Aslet and to see them through his eyes. I could not be more grateful for all his generous text, energy and enthusiasm and indeed for the wonderful photographs that Dylan Thomas has taken. I have greatly enjoyed getting to know him, Kate Turner and Ines Cross at Triglyph Books over the course of preparing this book.

Before I won a place on HRH The Prince of Wales's Summer School in 1990 I thought I was the only architecture student in the world who was interested in traditional design. Those few weeks changed my life, introducing me to a global network of like-minded people; providing me with the opportunity to share some of my design interests with students at The Prince of Wales's School of Architecture and elsewhere and, more recently, to serve as Masterplanner and Duchy architect at Nansledan and on the Kennington Estate in London. Throughout those three decades His Royal Highness The Prince of Wales, now His Majesty King Charles III, has been both an inspiration and has afforded me unparalleled opportunities. I could not be more grateful, and was delighted when, in early 2022, His Majesty, as the then and now Former Prince of Wales, kindly agreed to write the foreword to *Living Tradition*.

My dear parents sadly died before I really got going as an architect. My enthusiasm for buildings was kindled by them both at a tender age. How I wish I could give them a copy of this book: I hope that they would approve?

And finally, I must acknowledge my debt to my darling wife Chloë for her love, devotion and unswerving support at all times, and for our two wonderful children, Harry and Charlotte who are the centre of our world.

PICTURE CREDITS

All images © Dylan Thomas except the following:

10/11 © Hugh Hastings
18 left © Richard Ivey
18 right © Andrew Wallace Hadrill
19 © Hugh Petter
22 © Ian Wallman
45-49 © Paul Barker
52-55 © Paul Barker
57-60 © John Critchley
63-71 © Scott Frances
79 © John Minshaw
129-138 © Paul Barker
214-215 © Ian Wallman
229 © Morley Von Sternberg
250/251 © Hugh Hastings
256 © Hugh Hastings
257 © Hugh Hastings
262 © Hugh Hastings
267 © Hugh Hastings
272 © Hugh Hastings
276/277 © Glass Canvas
284/285 © Glass Canvas
296-298 © Chris Draper
301 © Hugh Petter
303 top left © Hugh Petter
303 bottom left © Hugh Petter
303 bottom right © John Critchley
304 top left © Hugh Petter
304 bottom left © Hugh Petter
305 top left © Philip Blackwell
305 bottom left © Hugh Petter
306 column two © ADAM Architecture
306 column three © Glass Canvas
307 column one top © Hugh Petter
307 column one bottom © ADAM Architecture
307 column three top © John Critchley
308 column two © Future Publishing Ltd
308 column three © Richard Symonds
309 column one top © Marianne Majerus
309 column one bottom © ADAM Architecture
309 column three © Hugh Petter
310 column two top © Paul Highnam
310 column two bottom © Tim Gray
310 column three top © ADAM Architecture
310 column three bottom © Paul Barker
311 column one top © Paul Highnam
311 column one middle © Paul Barker
311 column one bottom © Paul Highnam
311 column three top © Paul Highnam
312 column one top © John Critchley
312 column one bottom © John Critchley
312 column two bottom © John Critchley
312 column three middle © Paul Highnam
312 column three bottom © John Critchley
313 column one © Douglas Martin
313 column two middle © Hugh Hastings
313 column two bottom © Chris Draper
314 column one © Tim Aylen
314 column two © ADAM Architecture
314 column three top © Chris Draper
314 column three middle © John Critchley
314 column three bottom © Laura Eperjesi
315 column one top © ADAM Architecture
315 column two top © ADAM Architecture
315 column two bottom © Seb Bone
315 column three © ADAM Architecture
316 © Joe Low
Back cover © Hugh Hastings

Every reasonable effort has been made to acknowledge the ownership of copyright for photographs included in this book. Any errors that may have occurred are inadvertent, and will be corrected in subsequent editions provided notification is sent in writing to the publisher.

First published in the United Kingdom in 2023 by Triglyph Books.

Triglyph Books
154 Tachbrook Street
London SW1V 2NE

www.triglyphbooks.com
Instagram: @triglyphbooks

Text copyright © 2023 Clive Aslet
Photography copyright © 2023 Dylan Thomas and other copyright holders: p319
Copyright © 2023 Triglyph Books

Designed by Steve Turner
www.steveturnerdesign.com

Publisher: Clive Aslet and Dylan Thomas
Production Manager: Kate Turner
Assistant Editor: Ines Cross
Editorial Assistant: Leona Crawford
Production Coordinator: Claire Mercer
Proofreader: Mike Turner

All rights reserved. No part of this publication may be reproduced, stored in a retrieval system, or transmitted in any form or by any means, electronic, mechanical, photocopying, recording, or otherwise, without prior consent of the publisher.

British Library Cataloguing-in-Publication Data.
A catalogue record for this book is available from the British Library.

ISBN : 978-1-9163554-5-3

Printed and bound sustainably in Italy.

Living Tradition

The Architecture and Urbanism
of Hugh Petter

TRIGLYPH
BOOKS